RYA VHF Handbook

by Tim Bartlett

Illustrations by Steve Lucas

Reprinted June 2010

© Tim Bartlett 2009
First Published 2006
The Royal Yachting Association
RYA House, Ensign Way, Hamble
Southampton SO31 4YA
Tel: 0844 556 9555
Fax: 0844 556 9516
Email: publications@rya.org.uk
Web: www.rya.org.uk
ISBN: 9781905104031
RYA Order Code: G31

Totally Chlorine Free **Sustainable Forests**

A CIP record of this book is available from the British Library

Note: While all reasonable care has been taken in the preparation
of this book, the publisher takes no responsibility for the use of the
methods or products or contracts described in the book.

Cover Design: Balley Design Limited
Photographic credits: Tim Bartlett, Chloe Phillips-Bartlett,
Icom UK, Johnson Controls Inc, Yaesu UK, Simrad UK, Raymarine,
MACGA, UK Hydrographic Office, ICS Electronics, SM Group (Europe),
McMurdo, Selex Communications and LightMaster Software.

Typeset: Creativebyte
Proofreading and glossary: Alan Thatcher
Printed in China through World Print

All prices shown are correct at the date of publication.

Contents

Syllabus item A1.1

Throughout this book you will find red boxes as shown above; these highlight which item of the RYA VHF Course Syllabus the section relates to.

1 Introduction

Ask any group of students attending an SRC course why they want to learn to use a marine VHF radio, and the overwhelming majority are likely to reply "safety". Probe a little deeper, and most of them will probably say that they want it mainly to be able to call for help.

Types of message

Syllabus item A1.1

It's true that distress messages are an important function of marine VHF, but they are certainly not its sole purpose: VHF can also be used to prevent distress situations from developing, by allowing vessels to warn each other of potential hazards, or by receiving safety information such as navigational warnings and weather forecasts.

The majority of radio messages, however, are far more mundane. They are concerned with everyday aspects of the vessel's operation: making plans, or finding berths, food, or fuel.

There is also a facility, in some countries but not in the UK, for specially equipped radio stations on the coast to connect radio calls to the public telephone system ashore. Unlike other calls made by VHF radio, these "link calls" have to be paid for. They were never cheap, so most of the customers who might once have used this service now use mobile telephones or satellite communications instead.

VHF may also be used for on-board communications, such as between the bridge and fo'c'stle of a ship, or between the cockpit of a yacht and someone working up the mast.

So the types of message that can be sent by marine VHF can be divided into four main groups:-

Distress, Urgency, and Safety messages

Routine messages   - between vessels
                            - between vessels and harbour authorities ("Port operations")
                            - between vessels and traffic monitoring or control authorities

Public Correspondence, or "Link calls"
On-board communications

Types of user

Syllabus item A1.2

The people who use marine VHF can also be divided into several distinct groups.

The largest group are those who use marine VHF on board a vessel of some sort, whether it is a yacht, fishing boat, ship or hovercraft. So far as the authorities are concerned, these are all classed as "Ship Radio Stations", regardless of whether the "ship" in question is a cruise liner or a canoe.

The other broad group of users are based ashore. They include Coastguards and other search and rescue organisations, as well as harbourmasters, pilots, marinas, and yacht clubs.

> Getting a licence to set up a coast radio station is more complicated and expensive than obtaining a ship radio licence, and it is subject to more restrictions on its use. You cannot just buy an ordinary marine VHF radio and set it up on your kitchen window sill!

Some aircraft, such as coastguard helicopters, also carry marine VHF equipment.

Types of equipment

A typical fixed radio consists of a compact box, with a display and control panel on the front, mounted either in a bracket or recessed into a bulkhead. It is powered by the vessel's electrical system, and has a separate antenna (aerial) mounted on a mast or on a high part of the superstructure.

A typical portable radio is smaller than a fixed radio but larger than a mobile phone. It is usually powered by a rechargeable battery fitted inside or clipped to it, and usually has a stubby antenna connected directly to the top of the radio.

Making waves

If you tap a screwdriver across the terminals of a 9-volt dry battery, it will produce tiny sparks. The sparks are difficult to see, except in complete darkness, but if you do it close to an ordinary transistor radio, they should be easy enough to hear, as a distinct crackle on the radio. That, in effect, is what Heinrich Hertz did in 1888, when he became the first person to demonstrate the existence of what we now know as radio.

The sparks create an electric field which builds up quickly but then collapses. This rapidly changing electric field generates a magnetic field, which also grows, and collapses. This combination of constantly changing electric and magnetic fields produces what we know as electromagnetic radiation, or radio waves.

More sophisticated radio transmitters work by supplying a rapidly changing electric current to an antenna (aerial) to create the electric field. The speed at which the current changes controls the speed at which the electric field around the antenna changes, and is measured in Hertz (usually abbreviated to Hz).

> 1 Hz = 1 cycle per second
> 1kHz = 1kiloHertz = 1 thousand cycles per second
> 1MHz = 1 Megahertz = 1 million cycles per second
> 1GHz = 1 Gigahertz = 1 billion cycles per second

If you find it difficult to visualize a fluctuating electric field, imagine, instead, that someone has just dropped a pebble into a pond. The pebble represents the transmitter, and the ripples radiating out from it represent the fluctuating electrical and magnetic field.

Frequency and wavelength

Syllabus item A1.3

One big difference between the waves on the pond and the electromagnetic waves of a radio transmission is that radio waves travel outwards in three dimensions, not just two. Another, even more important, is that all electromagnetic waves travel at 300,000,000 metres per second, (roughly 186,000 miles per second or 162,000 nautical miles per second).

300,000,000 metres per second is known as "the speed of light" because light is one of many kinds of electromagnetic wave.

Imagine that you can see electromagnetic waves as clearly as you can see the waves on the sea. You know that they are travelling at 300 metres per microsecond, so if 30 of them pass you in one microsecond, the first one must be 300 metres away by the time the thirtieth one has past you. From this, you can see that each wave must be 10 metres long. In other words, they have a wavelength of 10 metres. Similarly, If 300 of them pass you in 1 microsecond, they must have a wavelength of 1 metre.

> Wavelength = 300,000,000 / Frequency
> Frequency = 300,000,000 / Wavelength

> Marine VHF operates at a frequency of about 156MHz
> So it has a wavelength of about 300 / 156 = 1.92 metres.

Characteristics of different frequencies

Syllabus item A1.3

The electromagnetic spectrum covers a huge range of frequencies and wavelengths, from the audible "mains hum" generated in some mains-powered electrical equipment, to X-rays and gamma rays. Visible light is part of the spectrum, towards the upper end of the frequency range (from 384,000 GHz to 769,000 GHz).

Radio waves have much lower frequencies, from about 3kHz to 30GHz, and their wavelengths range from several kilometres to a few centimetres. Different frequencies have different characteristics, which make them suitable for different purposes, so they are often subdivided into different "bands", with descriptive names such as VLF (Very Low Frequency) and SHF (Super High Frequency).

> In general, lower frequencies are more susceptible to the effects known as diffraction and refraction, in which the waves are bent when they pass through or along the boundary between different media (such as between air and water).

This means that low frequencies (VLF and LF) are good for long range broadcasting and radio navigation systems, because they are easily diffracted, so they can curve around obstructions or over the horizon.

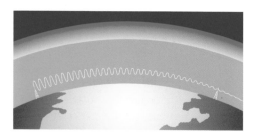

Medium frequencies (MF) are slightly less good at following the Earth's curvature, so they are used for some medium-range navigational aids, such as aeronautical radio beacons, for regional broadcasting, and for medium range communications.

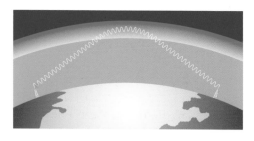

High frequencies (HF) don't bend over the horizon to any significant extent. The earth's atmosphere, however, contains a number of electrically-charged layers, known as the ionosphere. These layers are capable of refracting HF radio waves to such an extent that they bounce back to ground level. By carefully choosing the right frequency to make best use of the ionosphere, HF can be used for world-wide broadcasting and communication.

Very High Frequency (VHF) and Ultra High Frequency (UHF) don't bend over hills, around headlands, or over the horizon to any great extent, nor are they bounced back by the ionosphere, so they are used for local broadcasting, television, and communications.

The maximum range at which you can expect a VHF signal to be received depends on the height of the transmitting and receiving antennas.

> The distance to an antenna's VHF horizon (in miles) is approximately three times the square root of its height in metres.

Two antennas will be in within range of each other when their horizons overlap:

So a motor cruiser, with its antenna at 4m, would have a radio horizon of 6 miles, while a sailing boat, with its antenna at 16m, would have a radio horizon of 12 miles. They should be able to contact each other at a range of about 6+12=18 miles.

	Dinghy	Motor boat	Sailing yacht	Ship	Coast station
Antenna height	*1m*	*4m*	*16m*	*36m*	*100m*
VHF horizon	**3M**	**6M**	**12M**	**18M**	**30M**
Dinghy	6M	9M	15M	21M	33M
Motor boat	9M	12M	18M	24M	36M
Sailing yacht	15M	18M	24M	30M	42M
Ship	21M	24M	30M	36M	48M
Coast station	33M	36M	42M	48M	

Modulation

A constant, unchanging series of radio waves is of little practical use: it is the radio equivalent of a continuous single-note whistle, or a steady white light. In order to carry a message, it has to be varied in some way. This is known as "modulation", and in its simplest form consists of nothing more than switching the transmission on and off.

Simple on-off keying can be used to send messages by morse code or something similar, but more sophisticated forms of modulation are required to transmit sounds such as speech.

The first stage in the process is to convert sound — the physical vibration of the air — into electricity. This is the job of a microphone.

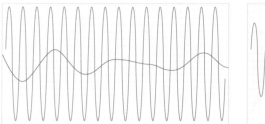
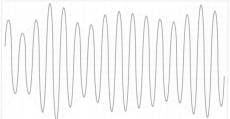

Amplitude Modulation: the sound waves (shown in red) modulate the radio "carrier wave" (shown in green) to produce a signal whose frequency and wavelength are constant, but whose amplitude ("height") varies.

It is then technically simple to use the electrical signal from the microphone to vary the amplitude (wave "height") of radio waves, while keeping their wavelength and frequency constant. This is known as Amplitude Modulation, or AM. It is used for MF broadcasting and a variation of it (Single Sideband, or SSB) is used in marine MF communications.

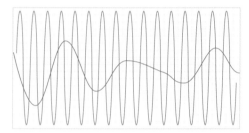
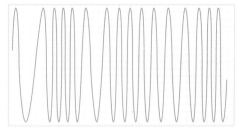

Frequency Modulation: the sound waves modulate the frequency of the carrier wave, rather than its amplitude.

A more complex, but technically superior alternative is to vary the frequency of the radio waves. This is known as Frequency Modulation, or FM, and is used for VHF broadcasts, and for VHF and UHF communications.

Antennas

Syllabus item B1.4

Almost all electrical and electronic equipment transmits and receives electromagnetic waves, whether it is intended to or not. A radio, however, is specifically intended to transmit and receive radio waves as efficiently as possible. To do so, it requires an antenna — sometimes called an aerial or occasionally a radiator.

The science behind how an antenna works is complex, but a key point is that a vertical antenna is most efficient if it is very slightly shorter than half the wavelength of the radio waves it is intended to transmit. The exact length varies slightly, depending on the diameter of the antenna, but for marine VHF, the optimum length is about 93cm. Longer or shorter antennas will work, so long as they are an exact and simple ratio of the ideal length.

Antenna gain

No practical antenna transmits equally in all directions. In simple terms, you can say that "the power comes out of the sides of the antenna, not out of the ends". So a long antenna, mounted vertically, will concentrate more of its power towards the horizon than a shorter one. This, of course, is very useful if you can guarantee that your antenna will be mounted vertically. If you can't, there is something to be said for using a shorter antenna, which is less effective at focusing its power towards the horizon, when it is vertical, but is more tolerant of being tilted.

To help choose an antenna, manufacturers usually specify the "gain" of their different models, compared with a theoretical "isotropic" antenna (which transmits equally in all directions). The gain is usually specified in decibels, in which every 3dB represents a doubling in maximum signal intensity: -

A **3dBi antenna** focuses twice as much power towards the horizon as an isotropic antenna, but is reasonably tolerant of heel and pitch: this is the type usually recommended for sailing yachts.

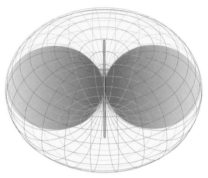

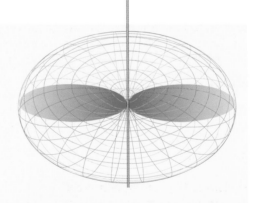

A **6dBi antenna** focuses twice as much power towards the horizon as a 3dB antenna, or four times as much as an isotropic antenna, but its efficiency drops off noticeably if it is tilted, so it is usually recommended for motorboats — but only if it can be mounted upright.

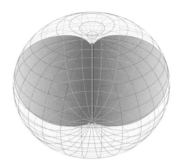

A **1.5dBi antenna** is less effective at concentrating its power in any particular direction, but, by the same token, is not too badly affected by being used at an angle. This is useful for portable radios.

The "feeder" cable connecting the antenna to the radio is an important part of the whole system. The cable used for domestic televisions and radios may look the same as is used for marine VHF antennas, but its electrical properties are quite different, and will severely detract from the antenna's performance.

Batteries

Syllabus item A1.4

Marine VHF radios are almost invariably powered by batteries, whether they are internal, as in most portables, or are the boat's domestic batteries.

All batteries work by using chemical reactions to produce a flow of electrically charged particles, called electrons, in the circuit that links the battery's positive and negative terminals. The fundamental difference between rechargeable and non-rechargeable batteries is that in rechargeables, the chemical reactions can be reversed by pushing the electrons back through the battery in the opposite direction.

Alkaline batteries are not normally rechargeable, but they are readily available, and store a lot of power for their size and weight. Although they are not an economical option for regular, long-term use, they are a very useful reserve power supply for some portables that are designed to accept them.

Lithium batteries are expensive, and not rechargeable, but they produce a lot of power for their size and weight, and have a very long shelf life. This makes them ideal for emergency equipment such as EPIRBs or for portable radios which are reserved for emergency use. Like alkaline batteries, they produce 1.5 volts per cell when new.

Lead-acid batteries are very heavy and bulky, but they are rechargeable, and are produced in large sizes that make them an economical way of storing a lot of power. Not surprisingly, they are the standard type of battery for engine starting and domestic services on boats.

There are numerous variations. "Heavy Duty" batteries ("car batteries") will provide huge currents for very short periods, so they are ideal for engine starting, but they quickly deteriorate if they are discharged by more than about 30% of their capacity. "Deep cycle" or "traction" batteries are much better at withstanding deep discharges, but cannot provide such large currents, so they are better for supplying domestic power. "Leisure" batteries are an economical compromise between the other two types.

These "conventional" lead-acid batteries, supplying power to a vessel's main fixed VHF set, can be conveniently kept at a reasonable state of charge by the boat's engine-driven alternator. It isn't perfect, but it is a common and very practical solution.

More sophisticated versions of lead-acid batteries are filled with an acid gel or acid-impregnated mats instead of the liquid acid that is used in a typical car battery. This makes them less susceptible to spills or damage, but in most cases reduces their ability to produce very high currents (such as for engine starting) or to accept rapid recharging.

The chargers for the more sophisticated types of lead acid battery should be built into the boat when the batteries are installed. They may provide a slower rate of charge than normal, but they are designed to make sure that the battery really is fully charged.

NiCad (Nickel Cadmium) batteries are compact and rather lighter than lead acid batteries, but they are more expensive, so they are mainly used in small sizes to power portable radios. They are potentially able to withstand thousands of charge/discharge cycles, but they are inclined to lose their charge gradually when stored and their ability to accept a full charge quickly deteriorates due to the so-called "memory effect" if they are subjected to "top-up" recharging without having been fully discharged. They produce a slightly lower voltage than alkaline batteries, so some equipment designed to accept alkalines will not work with NiCads.

NiMH (Nickel Metal Hydride) batteries are rechargeable, and have a higher capacity than NiCads of similar size and weight, as well as being able to deliver more current. They don't last quite as long as well-maintained NiCads, but the "memory effect" is very much less significant. Unfortunately, they produce the same low voltage as NiCads, but they are more expensive and are inclined to self-discharge even when not used.

Lithium Ion batteries are rechargeable. For a given size and weight, they store more power than any other readily-available battery, but are very much more expensive, and very much more susceptible to overcharging.

Recharge NiCads only when they are flat

Top up other rechargeables whenever you can

Don't overcharge any rechargeable, but particularly not a Lithium Ion.

Don't recharge alkalines or lithiums

Rules and Regulations

Why rules?

Radio waves are no respecters of borders, whether the border in question is the fence between next door neighbours, or an international frontier. To stop one family's baby alarm from making their neighbour's garage door fly open, and prevent one country's television broadcasts from disrupting the air traffic control systems of another, calls for some degree of co-operation.

Co-operation is achieved through the International Telecommunication Union (ITU). Every two to three years, it organises a World Radio Conference (WRC), attended by delegations representing nearly two hundred different countries. The outcome of each conference is an update to the Radio Regulations — an international treaty whose requirements must then be incorporated into the national legislation of every state that has signed up to it.

The more general activities of ships and boats are regulated at international level by the International Maritime Organisation (IMO). This is the body responsible for — amongst other things — the collision regulations, the layout of traffic separation schemes, and the Safety of Life at Sea (SOLAS) Convention.

Within the UK, two government bodies are particularly concerned with the administration and enforcement of the laws relating to marine VHF:

The Office of Communications (Ofcom) deals mainly with technical issues, and matters arising from the radio regulations, such as whether a radio installation is licensed.

The Maritime and Coastguard Agency (MCA) deals mainly with matters arising from SOLAS, such as whether a vessel is carrying the right equipment and whether the operator is appropriately qualified.

Penalties for infringing the Radio Regulations can be severe: they include fines of up to £5000, up to six months imprisonment, and confiscation of the equipment used.

Licensing

In order to use a VHF radio on board a boat, two quite different types of licence are required:-

A Ship Radio Licence
An Authority to Operate

Ship Radio Licences

A Ship Radio Licence could be compared to a car's tax disc, in that it relates to the vessel or to the radio, rather than to an individual user, and it has to be regularly renewed. Until 30 September 2006, comparisons with a tax disc were even more obvious: obtaining a licence involved paying an annual fee, in exchange for a circular licence disc which had to be displayed on board.

Under the new rules, Ship Radio Licences are issued free by Ofcom through their website (www.ofcom.org.uk), and will remain valid for up to ten years, so long as the details of the vessel and its owner don't change. If the boat is sold, the owner's address changes, or the radio equipment is changed, the licence will have to be renewed. There is no longer a "licence disc", but the licence must be carried on board.

Although the licence is free, it is still compulsory, and owners may be fined for having operational radio equipment on board without an appropriate licence.

A Ship Fixed Radio Licence covers all the radios installed on a vessel, including a portable used in the vessel's tender.

When a vessel is issued with a Ship Radio Licence for the first time, it is allocated a callsign, consisting of a group of four or five letters and numbers, and it may also be given a nine-digit MMSI number.

Essentially, the callsign and MMSI number are both unique identifiers that will stay with the vessel until her radio licence is allowed to lapse. So although there may be several boats called *Colossal Overdraft*, there will only be one that has the callsign *MVYQ8* or the *MMSI 234014521*.

The difference is that the MMSI is used in conjunction with Digital Selective Calling (DSC, see pages 62-63), whereas the callsign is essential if you ever want to use the link call facility, and useful if you want some authority such as the Coastguard to be able to identify you quickly and positively.

A Ship Portable Radio Licence covers only one portable radio, and does not include the issue of a callsign. The main difference between this and a ship radio licence is that it licences the **radio** rather than the **vessel**, so it is useful for people such as instructors and delivery skippers, who may well have a portable that they want to be able to use on any boat.

Coast Station Licences

Syllabus item D2.2

Shore-based premises, such as marinas and sailing clubs will not be issued with ship radio licences, even though they have a legitimate need to use marine VHF. To cater for them, there are a number of different types of Coast Station Licences.

Coast Station Licences are also issued by Ofcom but they are not free and are subject to more stringent limitations than Ship Radio Licences.

Coastal Station Radio (UK) licences are used by organisations, which need to be able to communicate between a base station and their own vessels using a "private" channel. The fee for a CSR(UK) Licence is £180 per channel per year.

Coastal Station Radio (International) licences are used mainly by harbour authorities and the like, to communicate between a base station ashore and any vessel with a conventional marine VHF, using one or more designated channels (frequencies). The licence fee is £100 per channel per year.

Coastal Station Radio (Marina) licences are useful for sailing clubs as well as for commercial marinas, as they allow the use of three channels (M, M2, and 80) for the relatively modest fee of £75 per year.

Coastal Station Radio (Training School) licences are for exactly what the name suggests: they allow maritime colleges and training centres to use "live" marine radio equipment, for training purposes only, for a fee of £50 per year.

Maritime Radio (Suppliers and Demonstration) licences also cost £50 per year, and allow businesses to install, test, repair and demonstrate marine radios in their shops or workshops and on customers' boats in harbour or ashore.

Authority to Operate

Syllabus item D2.2

The Authority to Operate is like a driving licence: it relates to an individual, rather than to a specific vessel or radio; it is awarded after a test of competence, and it lasts — at least in theory — for life.

There are several different courses and examinations, providing a range of qualifications that give "authority to operate" radio equipment of different sorts, on different classes of vessel. Someone who has completed a one-day course in using a small-boat's VHF, and taken a half-hour written test is not expected to take responsibility for the world-wide communication needs of a ship carrying a thousand passengers!

For vessels which carry radio equipment on a voluntary basis there are two certificates:-

the Long Range Certificate (LRC) - covers VHF, HF, and MF radiotelephony and satellite communication systems

the Short Range Certificate (SRC) - covers VHF radiotelephony.

Under UK law, "Voluntary fit" vessels includes those whose owners have "chosen" to conform to the Codes of Practice for small commercial craft

Type approval

Until April 2000 anyone who wanted to sell a marine radio had to make sure that it had been tested by an independent test facility and approved as conforming to various performance requirements.

Since April 2000, that requirement has been replaced by the European Radio and Telecommunications Terminal Equipment Directive (the R&TTE Directive). The principle is the same: radio equipment has to do its job without being dangerous and without causing unnecessary interference, but the test requirement has gone. The manufacturer now has to issue a **declaration of conformity**, formally certifying that the radio conforms to the appropriate performance standards, and ensure that it is marked with the familiar CE label.

An alternative — compulsory for SOLAS vessels — is that the radio should conform to the type approval requirements of the Marine Equipment Directive (MED) and be marked with the "ship's wheel" symbol.

Strictly speaking, it is up to the holder of the ship radio licence to make sure that the radio equipment conforms to all these requirements. In practice, it is almost impossible for anyone to do so, without a high level of technical knowledge and access to sophisticated test facilities. If you have access to the documentation supplied with the radio when it was first bought, look for a copy of the declaration of conformity. Otherwise, look for the CE mark or ship's wheel mark.

Be careful of radios imported from outside Europe, bought by mail order (particularly from websites) or bought at boat jumbles. Many radios, especially those built for the American market, do not conform to the European standards. They are not necessarily "sub standard" but it is illegal to install one under the terms of a UK Ship Radio Licence.

Radio log
Syllabus item D2.2

The Radio Regulations require all vessels with radio telephone equipment to keep a record of distress, urgency, and safety messages received or sent, along with other "important events" concerning the radio, and a daily note of the ship's position. Under UK law, pleasure craft, and small commercial craft operating under any of the MCA Codes of Practice, are exempt from this requirement. It is still, however, good practice to make a note of such events in the boat's deck log when required.

Secrecy
Syllabus item D2.2

Anything you say over a marine VHF radio can be picked up by anyone with another ordinary marine radio within a radius of many miles. In some respects, this is a great strength: one distress message, for instance, may be he heard by hundreds of other vessels, without having to be repeated to each one in turn. It does, however, mean that radio operators are duty bound to respect the confidences of their counterparts.

The need for secrecy is enshrined in the international Radio Regulations, in British law, and in the declaration of secrecy that is included in the application for a radio operator's certificate.

It is a criminal offence to:-

   Intercept radiocommunications not intended for the general use of the public without authorization

   Divulge the existence or contents of any information obtained by the interception of radio communications.

> In other words:-
> Don't eavesdrop   Don't gossip

The ten commandments

Syllabus item C3.3; D2.2v

The complete text of the Radio Regulations fills four substantial books. Even the reduced version, edited down to leave only the bits that refer to marine radio, is an A4 book about 2cm thick. The most important rules, however, can be reduced to ten commandments:-

Do not transmit without the authority of the master of the vessel

Do not transmit false or deceptive distress or safety signals

Do not transmit without identification (callsign or vessel name)

Do not shut down a radio telephone before finishing all operations resulting from a distress, urgency, or safety call

Do not broadcast, other than distress messages

Do not transmit music

Do not make unnecessary transmissions

Do not transmit profane, indecent or obscene language

Do not use unauthorized frequencies

Do not transmit messages intended to be received ashore, other than by a licensed coast radio station.

Most of these are pretty self-explanatory, except, perhaps for "Do not broadcast" and "Do not make unnecessary transmissions". Almost by definition, everyone else's radio messages always seem to be unnecessary chatter, compared with your own!

"Broadcasting" means transmitting a message without specifying who it is intended for and without expecting a reply.

A simple rule of thumb test of whether a message is "necessary" is "does this message relate to the ship's business?"

So two fishermen discussing the day's catch would be OK; a discussion of the results of last night's football match would not.

A group of divers discussing the nearest source of diving air would be acceptable; discussing the difficulties of towing a RIB around the M25 would not.

Yachtsmen are often accused of cluttering the airwaves with chit chat. A conversation which starts with a discussion agreeing to rendezvous with a friend in a particular harbour can easily slide through a comparison of local pubs to a discussion of their menus or reminiscences of what happened last time they met.

Arranging a rendezvous is obviously an acceptable use of the radio, but reminiscing about an evening ashore, equally clearly, is not.

Operating a marine VHF radio

Syllabus item B1.2

Every make and model of marine VHF radio is different. Whilst there may be a certain family resemblance between different models from one manufacturer, or between competing products aimed at the same group of users, there is certainly no such thing as a "standard" control panel. There are, however, a number of standard controls:-

Power on
Volume
Squelch
Transmitter power
Channel selector
PTT switch
Dual watch/Tri watch/Scan
Dimmer

Power on

The power on/off switch connects the radio to its power supply, so until it has been switched on, the radio is useless.

In fixed mount radios, the power on/off switch is often a press-button, mounted on the front panel. In hand-held portables, it is often combined with the volume control.

Volume

The function of the volume control is exactly the same as that of its counterpart on a domestic radio or television: it makes the sound from the loudspeaker either louder or softer.

Some radios, particularly those with telephone-style handsets, have a "mute" facility, which switches the loudspeaker off altogether when the handset is removed from its cradle.

Squelch

The squelch control regulates the sensitivity of the receiver, so it affects the radio's ability to receive incoming signals. It does not, however, affect the volume of the audio signal heard through the loudspeaker or handset.

Turning the squelch "up" reduces the sensitivity of the receiver and vice versa. When the squelch is turned right down, the receiver will detect a lot of very weak signals, including "static" and atmospheric noise, which will produce a sharp crackling, or frying sound through the loudspeaker. This is a very useful indicator of whether the volume control is set to about the right level, but no-one would put up with it as background noise for very long.

As the squelch control is gradually turned up, there will come a point at which the noise suddenly stops. This is the correct setting: the receiver has been desensitised sufficiently to eliminate unwanted signals, but should still be able to receive wanted signals.

Turning the squelch up further will desensitise the receiver still more, and runs the risk of losing weak signals.

Transmitter power

The maximum power that can be legitimately transmitted by a marine VHF radio is 25 watts. That doesn't sound very much, compared with something like a domestic light bulb, but in the right conditions and from a tall enough aerial, it may be good for a range of sixty miles or more.

For short range communications, there is no need to use so much power: perfectly satisfactory results can be achieved with much less. Of course, this reduces the drain on the battery, but the really big advantage of using less power is that by reducing the range over which one vessel's transmissions can be heard, it allows others, a few miles away, to use the same frequency.

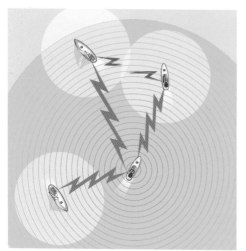 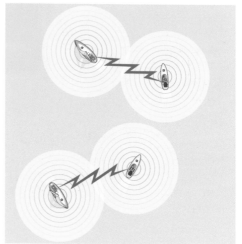

One selfish operator using high power can disrupt other vessels' communications over a wide area. Using low power allows other vessels a few miles away to use the same channel.

For this reason, all marine VHF radios must be able to transmit on a reduced power setting of 1 watt or less. With a good aerial, at least a couple of metres above the waterline, even this may achieve good communication over distances of 5-10 miles.

Portable VHF sets could, in law, transmit at up to 25 watts, but in practice they never do. In most cases, their maximum output is between 3 watts and 6 watts, but they are still required to have a 1 watt low power facility.

Channel selector

In order for one radio to receive the signals transmitted from another, the transmitter and receiver have to be tuned to the same frequency as each other. VHF frequencies, however, involve long and unmemorable sequences of numbers, such as 156.375 Mhz. To simplify things, some frequencies have been given international channel numbers (see page 25). 156.375MHz, for instance, is known as Channel 67.

Being able to change channel quickly and accurately is so important that on most radios, the channel selector is the most prominent control. It's usually in the form of a rotary knob or up and down keys, and matched by prominent numbers on the display, but in some cases — generally the more up-market models — it may be a numbered keyboard.

Channel 16 is of particular significance, because it is used for distress and safety messages, and for making initial contact with other vessels, so many radios have a separate control giving instant access to Channel 16 at the press of a single button.

PTT switch

Perhaps the most important control of all is known as the PTT (Press-To-Talk) or Pressel switch. It is usually mounted on the side of the microphone or in the middle of the handgrip of a telephone-style handset. On portable radios, it is usually set into the side of the casing, alongside the display.

It does exactly what its name suggests: you have to press it in order to switch the radio from receive mode to transmit. By the same token however, it could be called (but isn't!) an RTL switch, for "Release to Listen", because you have to release it in order to receive.

Dual watch, Tri watch, and Scan

Channel 16 has special status as the distress, safety, and calling channel, so we are encouraged to keep a continuous "listening watch" on it. Other channels have other designated purposes. Channel 13 for instance, is used for "Bridge to Bridge" safety communications, while Channel 12 is a port operations channel. So a yacht crossing the English Channel may want to monitor Channel 13 as well as Channel 16 in the shipping lanes, and Channels 12 and 16 as she approaches Southampton.

All radios now have a Dual Watch facility, which allows them to monitor Channel 16 and any other designed channel. It doesn't, strictly speaking, monitor both channels at once. Essentially, the receiver is tuned mainly to Channel 16, but occasionally flicks over to the other channel. If it receives a signal on the other channel, it stay "locked on" to it: if not, it quickly flips back.

Some manufacturers have taken this idea a stage or two further, and offer tri watch (three channels) or scanner modes, (lots of channels).

> You cannot transmit while in dual watch mode: some radios switch dual watch off automatically when the PTT switch is pressed. Others simply do not transmit until dual watch has been switched off.

Dimmer

All radios need an illuminated display and controls if they are to be worked at night. A bright screen, however, can be dazzling, so any radio should have lighting that can be reduced or increased as required.

Switching on and setting up

Suppose we want to make a call to a marina, a couple of miles away, on Channel 80.

1.	Switch the power supply to the radio on
2.	Adjust the dimmer switch if necessary, to illuminate the display and controls
3.	Turn the squelch right down, to produce a frying sound from the loudspeaker
4.	Adjust the volume control until the frying sound is loud but tolerable
5.	Adjust the squelch control until the frying sound just stops
6.	Use the channel selector to select Channel 80
7.	Select low transmitter power
8.	LISTEN, to make sure the channel is not in use
9.	Press the PTT to speak
10.	Release the PTT to listen for a reply.

VHF Channels

Principle of "channels"

Syllabus item A1.3

For one radio to receive the signals transmitted by another, the receiver has to be tuned to the same frequency as the transmitter. To receive BBC Radio 4 broadcasts in the long wave, for instance, a receiver has to be tuned to 198kHz.

Higher frequencies, however, involve bigger and bigger numbers, until by the time we reach the VHF band, they are becoming unwieldy and difficult to remember. To save us having to cope with numbers such as 161.625 Mhz, the standard frequencies approved by the ITU have been given channel numbers.

Channel Designators	Transmitting frequencies (MHz)		Inter-ship	Port operations		
	Ship stations	Coast stations		Single frequency	Two frequency	Public Corresp.
60	156.025	160.625			✓	✓
01	156.050	160.650			✓	✓
61	156.075	160.675			✓	✓
02	156.100	160.700			✓	✓
62	156.125	160.725			✓	✓
03	156.150	160.750			✓	✓
63	156.175	160.775			✓	✓
04	156.200	160.800			✓	✓
64	156.225	160.825			✓	✓
05	156.250	160.850			✓	✓
65	156.275	160.875			✓	✓
06	156.300		✓			
66	156.325	160.925			✓	✓
07	156.350	160.950			✓	✓
67	156.375	156.375	✓	✓	HMCG SAR	
08	156.400		✓			
68	156.425	156.425		✓		
09	156.450	156.450	✓	✓		
69	156.475	156.475	✓	✓		
10	156.500	156.500	✓	✓	Oil Pollution	
70	156.525	156.525	Digital selective calling for distress, safety and calling			
11	156.550	156.550		✓		
71	156.575	156.575		✓		
12	156.600	156.600		✓		
72	156.625		✓			
13	156.650	156.650	✓	✓		
73	156.675	156.675	✓	✓	HMCG SAR	
14	156.700	156.700		✓		
74	156.725	156.725		✓		

Channel Designators	Transmitting frequencies (MHz)		Inter-ship	Port operations		
	Ship stations	Coast stations		Single frequency	Two frequency	Public Corresp.
15	156.750	156.750	✓	✓	Also on-board coms	
75	156.775					
16	156.800	156.800	DISTRESS, SAFETY AND CALLING			
76	156.825			✓		
17	156.850	156.850	✓	✓	Also on-board coms	
77	156.875			✓		
18	156.900	161.500		✓	✓	✓
78	156.925	161.525			✓	✓
19	156.950	161.550			✓	✓
79	156.975	161.575			✓	✓
20	157.000	161.600			✓	✓
80	157.025	161.625	Also Marinas etc UK only	✓	✓	
21	157.050	161.650			✓	✓
81	157.075	161.675			✓	✓
22	157.100	161.700			✓	✓
82	157.125	161.725		✓	✓	✓
23	157.150	161.750			HMCG SAR/MSI	
83	157.175	161.775		✓	✓	✓
24	157.200	161.800			✓	✓
84	157.225	161.825		✓	HMCG SAR/MSI	
25	157.250	161.850			✓	✓
85	157.275	161.875		✓	✓	✓
26	157.300	161.900			✓	✓
86	157.325	161.925		✓	HMCG SAR/MSI	
27	157.350	161.950			✓	✓
87	157.375			✓		
28	157.400	162.000			✓	✓
88	157.425			✓		
AIS 1	161.975	161.975				
AIS 2	162.025	162.025				

A larger version of these charts is shown on pages 82-83

Until the development of solid state electronics, VHF radios were relatively expensive, and not particularly widely used, so the part of the radio spectrum allocated to marine VHF was divided into 28 international channels, 50kHz (0.05MHz) apart and numbered from 1 to 28.

By the 1970s, however, the price of VHF had fallen and its popularity had risen, so those existing channels were becoming very crowded. Technology had also moved on, so the channel spacing of 50kHz seemed unnecessarily generous. The number of channels could be almost doubled, without using any more of the radio spectrum, by interleaving new channels between the old ones. So Channels 60 to 88 were added.

As well as having a designated frequency (or, in some cases two designated frequencies), each channel also has a specified purpose. Channel 12, for instance, is a Port Operations Channel. It would be physically possible for two boats to communicate with each other on Channel 12, but it would be disruptive, potentially dangerous, and definitely illegal to do so.

Simplex and duplex channels

Syllabus item A1.3

If two people want to talk to each other, it seems to make sense for them both to use the same frequency. There is, however, one slight snag with this idea…

When you are using one frequency, you can either receive, or transmit. You can't do both at once. Even if you had two separate radios and aerials, you still couldn't receive the other boat's transmissions at the same time as you were transmitting yourself, because your own transmissions would drown out those from the other vessel.

So using a single-frequency channel demands a degree of discipline and standard procedures to decide who is to talk and who is to listen, and how they are to switch roles when necessary to achieve two-way communication. The principle, however, is simple, so this method of operating on a single frequency is known as **simplex**, and the single-frequency channels are known as simplex channels.

Simplex operation is all very well between two operators who know what they are doing, and understand the limitations of a simplex channel. It is far less satisfactory if, for instance, you are using VHF to make a link call to your office, or to wish your mother in law a happy birthday.

If you are talking on the telephone to someone who remains totally silent, you very quickly begin to wonder whether there is something wrong with the phone! That's because normal conversation is a constant, two way process, even if one party does little more than grunt.

Normal, two-way conversations can be achieved by radio, by using two frequencies. One station transmits on one frequency, while the other transmits on the other. Of course, they must both have their receivers set up to receive the frequency that the other is transmitting.

This two-way, two-frequency operation is known as **duplex**, so the two-frequency channels are known as duplex channels. They are used, in the main, for public correspondence (link calls), for which two-way traffic is essential, and for some port operations channels.

You can compare the flow of radio traffic in simplex and duplex channels to the flow of traffic along a road:-

A simplex channel is like a single track road: traffic can only flow in one direction at a time, and two way traffic can only be achieved by taking it in turns

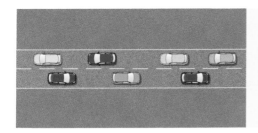

A duplex channel is like a two-lane road, in which traffic can flow freely in both directions.

Channel 80 is a typical duplex channel, intended for port operations. Coast stations transmit on 161.625MHz, and receive on 157.025MHz. This means that two coast stations can never communicate with each other on channel 80, but that is OK because there is no reason they should ever try to do so. Similarly, ship radio stations transmit on 157.025MHz and receive on 161.625MHz. Again, ship stations can't communicate with each other on channel 80, but that is OK because they are not supposed to use it as an inter-ship channel.

Channel 80, however, is of particular significance to Small Craft, because in the UK, it is one of the three channels covered by the Coast Station (Marina) licence. It is, in effect, the "Small Craft Port Operations channel". The snag is that most of the relatively economical radios sold for small craft use have only one antenna connection. You can't receive through an antenna at the same time as you are transmitting through it, even on a duplex channel.

This doesn't stop us from using duplex channels. The radio simply switches from receiving on one frequency to transmitting on the other, and vice versa. It all happens automatically when you press or release the PTT switch, whenever a duplex channel has been selected. The one snag with this so-called "semi-duplex" operation is that it sacrifices the very thing that duplex channels were set up to achieve: for most practical purposes, it is exactly like using a simplex channel.

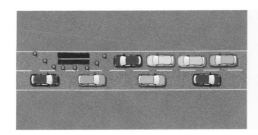

Semi-duplex operation can be compared to a two-lane road, with road works. The fact that one lane is blocked means that two-way traffic can only be achieved by taking it in turns, just as in a simplex channel.

International and private channels

Syllabus item A1.3

If you look carefully at the table of channel numbers, frequencies and approved usage on page 25, you'll see that there is quite a wide range of frequencies (from 157.450MHz to 160.600 MHz) that seem to be missing. That is because these frequencies have been left out of the international allocation, and have been set aside as "private" channels for individual governments to allocate as they think fit.

The UK government, for instance, allocates the name "00" to 156.000MHz, and allows it to be used only by the Coastguard and recognized search and rescue organisations such as the RNLI.

Similarly, in the UK, 157.850MHz is known as Channel M and 161.425 is known as M2: they are "private" channels that have been allocated by the UK government specifically for use by marinas, yacht clubs, and pleasure craft.

> Channel M and M2 should only be used in UK waters: other countries have allocated those frequencies for different purposes.

> Private channels do not necessarily require an operator's certificate. In the UK, channels M and M2 can be used by unqualified operators, without supervision.

> Some radios cannot display the letter M. In such cases, Channel M is often called "37" or "P1". Channel M2 is often called "P1" or "P4".

American channels

Syllabus item A1.3

A few countries, most conspicuously the USA, do not conform to the international channel designation and usage. Whilst there are similarities between international and US channel designations, there are also significant differences: in particular, many channels which are duplex in the international scheme are simplex in the US version. Most modern radios can be converted from one system to another by flicking a switch or by going through a set-up menu. Make sure you aren't using the wrong system by mistake.

> If you call a UK marina using the US channel 80, the marina will hear you, but you won't hear their reply. Channel 80 is a duplex channel under the international system, but a simplex channel in the USA.

Channel 16 and guard band

Syllabus item C3.5

Some channels are of particular significance.

Channel 16 is the outstanding example, because it is designated as the Distress, Safety, and Calling channel.

It is so important that Channel 16 should not suffer any interference that the two channels closest to it in the international frequency table — channels 75 and 76 — are regarded as a guard band. At one time, transmissions in the guard band were illegal, and any radio which allowed transmissions on those frequencies would fail its type-approval trials. The rules have now been relaxed very slightly, and these two channels are available for port operations use, but with the maximum power limited to 1 watt.

Calls on Channel 16 should be kept to a minimum, and apart from distress and safety calls, must never last longer than one minute.

Channel 70

Syllabus item C3.1

Channel 70 is the odd one out of all the international channels, because all the others are used for radiotelephony — the transmission of speech. Channel 70, however, is used for the transmission of digital data, in connection with digital selective calling (DSC).

DSC is covered in considerably more detail on pages 61 to 71. From the user's point of view, the important feature of Channel 70 is that it must never be used for voice transmissions.

Special channels

A few channels are of particular significance, and are worth memorizing.

0	A Private channel, designated in the UK for Search and Rescue organisations
6,8	Inter-ship channels
13	Used for direct bridge-to-bridge contact for matters of navigational safety
16	The Distress, Safety, and Calling channel
67	In the UK, used as a small craft safety channel
70	For DSC only — no voice transmissions allowed
72,77	Inter-ship channels
80	In the UK, the channel used by most marinas
M, M2	UK "private" channels dedicated to marinas, yacht clubs, and recreational craft.

Voice procedure 1: Routine calls

It may sound like a statement of the obvious, but radiotelephony is simply a method of communicating with a fellow human being by voice. Don't let the fact that there is a bit of electronic equipment involved blind you to that fact, or to the logical follow-up that in general you will communicate far more effectively by using plain straightforward English, with natural rhythms and intonation, than by using half-remembered jargon and distorted speech patterns.

Of course, the use of radio does involve a few constraints that are not present when you are simply chatting to friends:-

Listen, before you transmit, to make sure that you will not interfere with another call. Remember that VHF channels are a shared resource: there may be thousands of other vessels within radio range of you, all sharing one distress and calling channel and just four inter-ship channels.

Think before you speak. Plan what you are going to say and how you are going to say it.

Use the microphone correctly. If it is built into a telephone-style handset, hold it like a telephone. The more common fist mike, or a microphone built into a portable, should be held about 2-5cm from the mouth, but slightly off to one side to reduce the huffing and spitting noises that it will pick up if it is right in front of your lips.

Speak normally, or raise your voice very slightly, but don't shout, and try to speak at a normal, flowing speed. If you have a particularly high or low-pitched voice, or a pronounced accent, try to moderate it.

Press to talk and release to listen. One of the commonest mistakes by inexperienced operators is to forget to press or release the pressel switch when required. The last word you speak before you release the PTT switch should be "over" if you expect a reply, and "out" if you don't. "Over" means you expect a reply, and "Out" means you don't. "Over and Out" is contradictory, and can only mean that you are confused.

Identify yourself and who you are calling, using either your callsign or your boat name. This is obvious when you first make contact, but tends to get forgotten after the initial exchange. There is never any need to repeat names or callsigns more than three times, but it is important to include them at least once, every time you press the PTT switch.

Calling another vessel

Syllabus item D3.3

Suppose we are on *Snow White*, and want to arrange to meet the crew of *Rapunzel* in Helford this evening.

Channel 16 is the Distress, Safety, and Calling channel, so unless we have already made arrangements with *Rapunzel* to call her on some other channel, Channel 16 is obviously the one to use to make initial contact. We can't stay on Channel 16, though: we have an obligation to minimise our use of it, in order to keep it clear for other people. Having used it as a meeting place, we have to move away as soon as possible, to continue the conversation on a "working channel" earmarked for inter-ship calls. We also have an obligation to use low power if possible.

The first stage in the process, assuming the radio is already switched on and set up (see page 24) is to assess the situation. Is *Rapunzel* close enough to use low power? And which inter-ship channels are available?

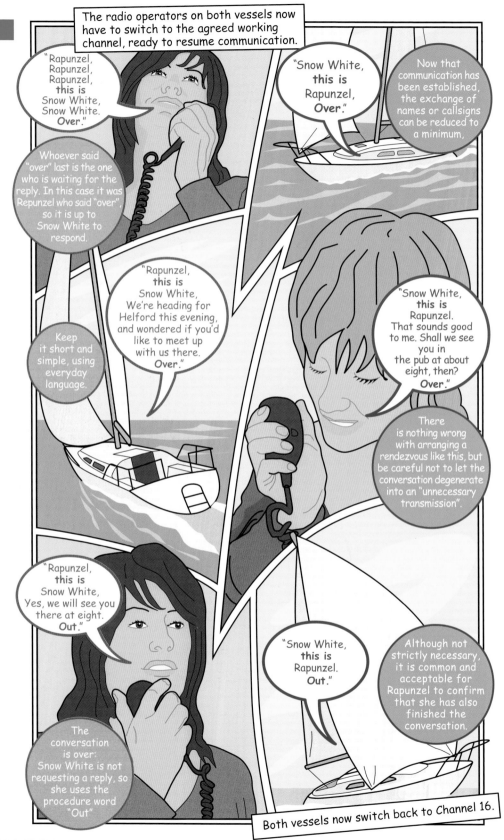

Calling a coast station

Syllabus item D3.3

The big difference between a coast radio station and a ship radio station is that the licence fee for a coast station costs more, and is based on a price per channel. So coast stations generally have as few channels as possible, and Channel 16 may not be among them.

The available channels (and the preferred working channel) for each station are published in various reference books, including the Admiralty List of Radio Signals, Admiralty Maritime Communications, and yachtsmen's almanacs.

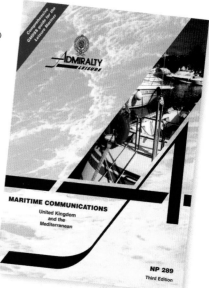

The procedure for calling a coast radio station, then, is very much the same as for calling another vessel, except that you should call directly on one of the station's specified working channels, rather than on Channel 16.

Suppose, for instance, that we are approaching Dover in the motor cruiser *Galadriel*, and would like permission to enter the harbour. Again, the first stage is to assess the situation.

The almanac shows that Dover Port Control operates on channels 74 and 12, with 74 as the preferred working channel. It is clear that there is not much point calling when we are more than a few minutes away from the entrance, so low power should be plenty.

Calling the Coastguard

Syllabus item D3.3

Coastguards, of course, are coast radio stations, but with a difference. They have a much wider range of channels available than other coast radio stations, and invariably include Channel 16 as one of the options.

In general, Coastguards should be called on Channel 16, as though they are another vessel. The choice of working channel, however, rests with the Coastguard.

One significant exception to this rule is Solent Coastguard, which, for routine matters, should be called on Channel 67.

Suppose, for instance, that we providing safety cover for a liferaft demonstration taking place in the Clyde, and the Coastguard have asked to be kept informed of its progress. As usual, the first stage is to assess the situation, and to listen to make sure that we are not about to interrupt another call.

"Clyde Coastguard, Clyde Coastguard, Clyde Coastguard, **this is** Gandalf, Gandalf, Gandalf, **Over.**"

"Gandalf, **this is** Clyde Coastguard. Channel six seven, please, six seven, and stand by. **Over.**"

It is always up to the coast radio station to choose the working channel. Coastguards usually choose 67.

"Clyde Coastguard, **this is** Gandalf Channel six seven, standing by. **Over.**"

Having changed the working channel, Gandalf waits for the coastguard to call back.

"Gandalf, **this is** Clyde Coastguard. **Over.**"

"Clyde Coastguard, **this is** Gandalf Just calling to tell you that we are about to start the liferaft demonstration off Largs Marina. **Over.**"

"Gandalf, **this is** Clyde Coastguard. Thank you for the information. Please let us know when you have finished. **Out.**"

"Clyde Coastguard, **this is** Gandalf Yes, we'll do that. Thank you. **Out.**"

Radio check

Syllabus item C3.4

Modern radios are generally reliable, and seldom fail suddenly for no reason, so simply using the radio as an everyday tool is a good check that it is working. Occasionally, however — after fitting a new antenna, for instance — you may need to make a test call.

A radio check can be carried out with any station that is prepared to co-operate, and on any channel on which they are listening. You could, for instance, call a marina or harbour office on its working channel, a friend's boat on some pre-arranged working channel, or the Coastguard on Channel 16 (Channel 67 in the Solent).

The procedure is simple:-

Garbled calls

Syllabus item D3.3

If you hear a call which is clearly intended for you, but you don't catch the name or callsign of the station it comes from, the solution is to reply to it as usual, but substituting the words station calling … for the unheard name or callsign:-

A more intractable problem arises when you hear a call which you think might have been for you, but you're not sure. In this case, there is no such easy answer: If you are not certain that the call was intended for you, do not answer it, because by doing so you might interfere with the reply from the person it was really meant for. If you ignore it for the time being, the station calling will undoubtedly repeat its call within a few minutes.

Unanswered calls

Syllabus item D3.3

A call that goes unanswered can be frustrating, but it is illogical to think that it will be answered if you repeat it immediately… or louder… or with more repetitions of the name or callsign.

If a call was ignored, it was probably because it wasn't heard or because the intended recipient was busy doing something else, so it makes sense to allow a distinct interval between calls, and to give up if several repeated efforts fail.

The radio regulations specify an interval of at least two minutes between attempts, and that you should only try three times before giving up. They do, however, allow you to start the sequence again three minutes later! Rather than simply waiting between successive attempts, it makes sense to see if there is some other reason why your call may not be getting through: make sure the antenna cable is connected, that the battery voltage is OK, and that the radio is correctly set up — not in dual watch mode, for instance, or with the volume turned right down!

Link calls

This once-useful facility, by which specially-equipped coast radio stations could link a VHF radio call from a vessel at sea to the shore telephone network, is falling into disuse as mobile telephones and satellite communications take over. Some countries, including the UK, Ireland, France and the Netherlands, have shut down their link call facilities altogether, but others — including Belgium, the Channel Islands, Denmark, Germany, Spain and Portugal — still have them. That, at least, was the situation in January 2007, but it does change, so look in a current almanac or list of radio signals for details.

Making a link call is not complicated: it is very much like making an operator-connected telephone call from a normal telephone. The most difficult bit is paying for it!

Link calls — Accounting procedures

Syllabus item D3.2

The very nature of marine communications means that a vessel from anywhere in the world may contact a coast radio station anywhere in the world, and ask to be connected to a telephone anywhere in the world. Somehow, the bills for all these telephone calls ultimately have to reach the right people.

If you think you may want to make a link call, you must first make arrangements with a Maritime Radio Accounting Authority (MRAA). There are several MRAAs in the UK. The Ship Radio Licence Guidance Notes (available from Ofcom) includes a list, but they are independent businesses whose terms and conditions vary: do not be surprised if they quote a fairly substantial deposit, or an annual subscription, as well as a surcharge on each bill.

Having signed up with an MRAA whose terms suit you best, their details, including a four character identity code known as the AAIC (Accounting Authority Identity Code), should be entered in the relevant space on your Ship Radio Licence application.

When you make a link call, the coast station that receives it will pass on the bill to your MRAA. Each MRAA pays all the bills it receives, but of course it also takes care to collate the all the bills relating to each vessel, and pass them on accordingly.

Link calls — Operating procedures

Syllabus item D3.1

Some coast radio stations accept incoming calls on Channel 16, but in general, they should be called on one of their working channels, listed in the Admiralty List of Radio Stations, Admiralty Maritime Communications, or yachtsmen's almanacs.

Before transmitting, however, it is important to listen to the channel, to make sure you do not interrupt someone else's call. You may hear:-

- an operator at the coast radio station, talking to another vessel
- one end of a telephone conversation
- various "telephone noises" such as clicks, squeaks, dialling or ringing tones
- a series of regular beeps
- or silence

Only if you hear silence can you go ahead with your call, using exactly the same procedure as if you were calling any other kind of coast radio station:-

The operator may well want to read back pieces of information, or ask you to repeat them, but will eventually say something to the effect that he is "trying to connect you", after which you will hear normal telephone noises, followed — if all goes well — by someone answering.

You are then able to go ahead with your call. When you have finished, call the coast radio station again, on the same working channel, to tell the operator that you have finished by the usual procedure: the word "out":-

• **Link calls — shore to ship** Syllabus item D3.1

It is possible, though increasingly unusual, for someone ashore to contact a vessel afloat by placing a link call through a coast radio station.

When the call is received by the coast radio station, it will add the details of the vessel called to its "traffic list", and broadcast a list of all those vessels on its current traffic list at a regular time given in the lists of radio stations and in yachtsmen's almanacs.

If you hear your own vessel name or callsign being called, it is up to you to call the coast radio station. The procedure is very much the same as if you instigate the call, except that instead of requesting a link call, you should say "you have **traffic** for me".

Prowords Syllabus item D1.5

Although it is generally best to avoid jargon, the examples of radio calls earlier in this chapter include several examples of special procedure words or "prowords":-

> this is
>
> over
>
> out
>
> radio check
>
> station calling
>
> say again
>
> I say again

To English-speakers, they look like everyday words, and their meanings are almost self-explanatory. In the international language of radio communications, however, they have quite distinct meanings which — like "over" and "out" — may be more tightly defined than in everyday speech.

All after All before	Used, for instance, when asking for part of a message to be repeated. If your pencil broke while writing down a shopping list, you might say "say again all after a pound of sausages"
Correct Wrong	"Correct" is used when someone has read back all or part of a message to confirm that it is correct. "Wrong" is used instead of "incorrect" because it sounds completely different, so it reduces the risk of confusion
Correction	Used when you have made a mistake, to put it right. So if you read a 116 carrots, then realised that it should have been 1lb (one pound) of carrots, you would say "a hundred and sixteen carrots, correction, one pound of carrots"
In figures In letters	Used to distinguish between letters and figures, where there is a risk of ambiguity, as between "Hawthorne Cottage, 5, Ashes Lane" and "Hawthorn Cottage, Five Ashes Lane"
I say again	I am going to repeat what I just said
I spell	I am going to spell the last word I said, using the phonetic alphabet
Out	This is the end of this transmission, and I do not expect a reply
Over	This is the end of this transmission, but I am expecting a reply
Radio check	Please comment on the strength and quality of my transmissions
Read back	Please read back to me the message that I have just passed to you
Received	I have received your message (not "roger")
Say again	Please say again what you just said
Station calling …	Used instead of a callsign or vessel name when you did not hear who was calling you
Text	Used to indicate the beginning of a message (such as a telegram) which you expect to be written down and relayed, verbatim, to someone else
Traffic	General term relating to radio communications
This is	Means "This is", when identifying yourself at the start of a call
Wait	Means "wait"! If possible, it should be qualified by giving some idea of how long you expect the other person to wait, as in "Wait five minutes"
Word after Word before	Used, for instance, when asking for a single word to be repeated or spelt out

Standard vocabulary

Syllabus item D1.5

English is regarded as "the international language" of the sea, so English speakers should have little difficulty understanding each other. Unfortunately this isn't always the case: there are differences in the words, as well as the accent, used in Orkney and Alderney, or even between the Royal and Merchant Navies.

In an effort to reduce confusion by encouraging the use of a "standard" English amongst seafarers around the world, the International Maritime Organization has introduced a standard marine navigational vocabulary.

Its use is not compulsory, but extracts from it are included in Appendix 2 (page 78).

Phonetic Alphabet

Syllabus item D1.6

The phonetic alphabet assigns a distinctive word to each letter of the alphabet, and to the numbers from zero to nine, to clarify spellings and minimise difficulties of language and pronunciation. Although you're unlikely to need to use the phonetic numbers around the coasts of Europe or Scandinavia, the phonetic letters are almost essential, particularly if you have a boat name whose spelling is likely to cause problems, such as *Pleiades* or *Bear Necessities*.

A	Alpha		N	November
B	Bravo		O	Oscar
C	Charlie		P	Papa
D	Delta		Q	Quebec
E	Echo		R	Romeo
F	Foxtrot		S	Sierra
G	Golf		T	Tango
H	Hotel		U	Uniform
I	India		V	Victor
J	Juliet		W	Whiskey
K	Kilo		X	X-Ray
L	Lima		Y	Yankee
M	Mike		Z	Zulu

1	Una One		6	Soxi Six
2	Bisso Two		7	Sette Seven
3	Terra Three		8	Okto Eight
4	Karte Four		9	Nove Niner
5	Panta Five		0	Nada Zero

Of all the reasons for wanting to have a radio on board, the ability to call for help in an emergency is undoubtedly at the very top of the list. It's important to appreciate, however, that a radio distress message may trigger an expensive, time consuming, and possibly dangerous search and rescue effort.

It is definitely not something to be used just because the wind has dropped and you would like a tow, or because the fuse has blown on your anchor winch.

> Strictly speaking, no radio transmission can be made without the authorization of the Master (or Skipper) of the vessel, but this is particularly true of distress calls. Even if the Master has delegated authority for authorising routine calls to someone else, distress calls must still be authorised by the person in charge of the vessel at the time.

Definition of distress

Syllabus item D1.1

The definition of "distress" under the Radio Regulations is rather narrower than in everyday language. In order to qualify as a distress situation:-

> a vessel, vehicle, aircraft or person
> must be in
> grave and imminent danger.

A dog has fallen overboard, and is in danger of drowning

The dog is in grave and imminent danger, but it is not a vessel, vehicle, aircraft, or person, so although this is a *distressing* situation, **it is NOT a distress situation**.

The skipper has fallen overboard, but you have practised the MoB routine lots of times.

It is far more difficult to recover a human being than to retrieve the fender and bucket used for practice, and survival after even a few minutes immersion in cold water is far from guaranteed. Unless you are 100% confident of a happy outcome, this incident involves grave and imminent danger to a person, so **it is a distress situation**.

A sailing boat has been dismasted, and the remains of the rig are tangled in her propeller. The strong wind is sweeping her quickly towards a rocky shore, only a mile or two away.

This concerns a vessel. It is in danger of being swept onto the rocks, and is likely to do so very soon. This meets both tests, so **it is a distress situation**.

A motor boat has been immobilised by discarded fishing gear tangled around her propellers and rudders. She is now drifting, some thirty miles from the nearest land.

This incident concerns a vessel, so it passes the first test. But although the vessel may eventually be in danger, it is certainly not imminent. This does not meet the "grave and imminent" test, so it is **NOT a distress situation**.

A sailing vessel has gone aground in a river estuary, on a falling tide, and is now stuck firmly in the mud.

This concerns a vessel, so it passes the first test, and the danger has already happened, so it is more than imminent. But there is no reason to believe that grounding on mud and in sheltered waters will involve the loss of the vessel, or endanger lives, so it fails to meet the "grave" part of the "grave and imminent" test, and **is therefore NOT a distress situation**.

After struggling to raise the anchor, the sixty year-old skipper suffered a severe pain in his chest, and fell to the deck.

These signs and symptoms could well indicate a heart attack. If someone on board is a doctor or paramedic, they might make a quick and confident diagnosis that it is really angina, and that the patient will soon recover. Someone with little or no first aid training could not be so confident, and would be justified in fearing the worst. **Whether this is a distress situation or not depends on the judgement of the person in charge of the vessel**. In this particular case, the "person in charge" is no longer the usual skipper.

The Distress Call

Syllabus item D1.1

The distress call is one of only two cases in which a ship radio station is allowed to broadcast: in other words, it is allowed to transmit a distress call and message without addressing them to anyone.

Although the Radio Regulations allow distress calls to be made on any channel, it clearly makes sense to use the channel that is set aside for the purpose, and to use the maximum power you have available.

> Select Channel 16
> Use High Power
> Remember to speak slowly and clearly

The distress call itself consists of the procedure word "Mayday", spoken three times, followed by the procedure words "this is" followed by your own boat name or callsign three times:-

> Mayday, Mayday, Mayday
> this is
> Princess Ida, Princess Ida, Princess Ida

Most of the prowords relating to distress are based on French.
Mayday itself comes from the French "M'aidez", meaning "help me!"

The Distress Message

Syllabus item D1.1

The distress call isn't addressed to anyone, and it doesn't include the word "over" to invite a reply. That is because it is intended to be immediately followed by the distress message.

The distress message always follows the distress call, but the two parts are quite separate and distinct:-

> the distress call is the initial "shout for help", intended to alert listeners to the coming message
>
> the distress message conveys important information to potential rescuers.

The distress message is intended to convey important information to potential rescuers. No-one is going to refuse to help you if you don't get it quite right, but you should still try to include the necessary information in the right order. This is partly because a practised routine is less likely to miss bits out, partly because the correct order puts the most important bits of information first, and partly because someone who doesn't speak very good English is more likely to understand what they hear if they receive the information in the order they are expecting.

It may help to write the nonsense word MIPDANIO on the edge of the chart, on the back of your hand, or to include it in a notice alongside the radio, because it is an acronym for the distress message.

M	Mayday	Even though you've just said Mayday three times in the distress call, say it again at the start of the distress message.
I	Identity	The boat name or callsign (just once, this time. It may be helpful to add a brief description, such as "yacht" or "motor cruiser" before the name. If you have sent a distress alert by DSC (see page 67), you should also include your MMSI.
P	Position	This is the single most important piece of information, but it can be sent in either of two ways (see page 47).
D	Distress	A brief explanation of what is wrong, such as "on fire" "aground" or "flooding". Don't waste time explaining how it happened.
A	Assistance	A brief explanation of what help you need, such as "request a tow", "request pumps", or "request helicopter evacuation". For most small craft incidents, any kind of help will do, so long as it comes quickly, so "request immediate assistance" would be most appropriate.
N	Number	The radio regulations say " any other information which might facilitate the rescue". The number of people involved is clearly relevant if, for instance, the boat is sinking or on fire, but less so if the incident concerns a man overboard or an injury. Don't waste time with ages, sexes, ranks or relationships.
I	Information	Apart from the number of people on board, this could include a brief description of the boat ("ten metre motor cruiser with a blue hull and white superstructure"), or your future intentions (we expect to abandon into a liferaft in five minutes").
O	Over	If ever you wanted a reply, this is it!

A complete distress call and message, then, goes like this:-

"Mayday, Mayday, Mayday, this is Princess Ida, Princess Ida, Princess Ida,"

"(M) Mayday.
(I) Motor Cruiser Princess Ida 232089001.
(P) My position is five zero degrees three two point three minutes north, three degrees, two five point four minutes west, on Adamant Sands.
(D) Aground.
(A) Request immediate assistance.
(N) Three people on board.
(I) Twelve metre motor cruiser, white deck and hull.
(O) Over."

With a little bit of luck, Princess Ida's distress call will soon be answered:-

"Mayday Princess Ida this is Brixham Coastguard, Brixham Coastguard, Brixham Coastguard, Received Mayday Over"

Notice that the reply to the distress call, and all subsequent radio messages connected with the distress incident, begins with the proword "Mayday". This gives absolute priority over all other transmissions - except, of course another Mayday.

Including the right items in the right order is important. In a real distress situation, it will help your rescuers to help you. In the SRC exam, a lot of students throw marks away by missing out the "Mayday" and "Identity" parts of the Distress mesage.

Specifying position

The obvious way to specify your position is by latitude and longitude, probably by reading it from the display of a GPS set. This is always acceptable, but it may not be the best option. In some situations, it should be treated with particular care.

> Check that the position indicated by the GPS is valid: if the GPS has been switched on within the past few minutes, or if its antenna has been damaged, it may not be showing the true position.

> If the battery voltage is low, such as by self-discharge through flood water or by continuously-running pumps, the added power drain of transmitting on the radio may lower the voltage so much that the GPS switches itself off.

Latitude and longitude are meaningless to a listener until they are plotted on a chart. To many local boats, something like "half a mile south of Gull Rock" or "the eastern side of Spit Sand" would mean a lot more. It is quite acceptable, and sometimes most appropriate, to give positions by reference to a well-known and charted landmark.

To conform to the International Marine Vocabulary, you should give the direction first, followed by the name of the landmark, and finally the distance:-

"My position is one six five degrees from Black Rock Buoy, two point four miles"

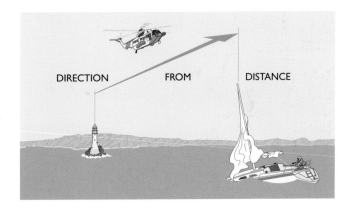

DIRECTION   FROM   DISTANCE

> Remember the order of things by imagining that you are giving directions to a helicopter pilot:- such as "fly south from the lighthouse for three miles".

> Remember that the hypothetical helicopter will be flying **from** the landmark **towards** you: make sure you don't send him the wrong way!

> Unless you specify otherwise, it will be assumed that bearings are in degrees true, and distances are in miles.

Receiving a distress message Syllabus items C3.2 and D1.1

It is a very well-established principle that seafarers are supposed to help each other when in distress. It is embodied in the international Safety of Life at Sea (SOLAS) convention, as well as in the Radio Regulations.

The ITU Convention says:-

Radio stations shall be obliged to accept, with absolute priority, distress calls and messages regardless of their origin, to reply in the same manner to such messages, and immediately to take such action in regard thereto as may be required.

That principle, however, needs to be diluted with a bit of common sense. If a cruise liner were to get into difficulties on its way out of Southampton on a summer Sunday, a thousand yachts and motor cruisers trying to reply to its distress call would not be exactly helpful!

More recent amendments to the Radio Regulations clarify the situation: in effect they say:-

if it is likely that a coast radio station (such as the coastguard) will have received the message, you should allow time for them to respond before doing so yourself

if you are not in a position to offer effective assistance, you should not acknowledge the message

unless you are acknowledging and assisting, you must maintain radio silence on any channel being used for distress communications.

As well as these compulsory requirements, it is a very good idea to write down as much of the distress message as possible, in case you subsequently find that you are able to assist in some way, such as by sending a Mayday Relay (see page 51)

Acknowledging a distress message

If, after several minutes, you have not heard a response from the coastguard, but decide that you are in a position to offer assistance, you should first acknowledge the distress call:-

"Mayday,
Princess Ida,
this is
Hilarion,
Hilarion,
Hilarion,
Received Mayday,
Out."

As soon as possible afterwards, follow up the acknowledgment by telling the casualty where you are, how fast you are travelling towards them, and when you expect to arrive:-

"Mayday
Princess Ida
this is
Hilarion,
Hilarion,
Hilarion,
My position is five zero degrees two nine point five minutes north, three degrees, two four point two minutes west. My speed two five knots. My ETA ten minutes. Out."

Seelonce

Syllabus item D1.1

The fact that there are distress communications going on, automatically imposes radio silence on the channel concerned. No-one, in other words, should transmit on that channel unless their message is directly connected with the distress incident or unless they are in distress themselves.

It is always possible, though, that someone may not realise that there is a distress incident in progress: they may have only just switched their radio on, or they may have only just arrived within range.

If this happens, the casualty or "the station in control of distress traffic" (such as the Coastguard) can remind anyone within range of the need for radio silence by using the prowords "Seelonce Mayday."

"All ships,
all ships,
all ships,
this is
Brixham Coastguard,
Brixham Coastguard,
Brixham Coastguard,
Seelonce Mayday,
I say again,
Seelonce Mayday,
Out."

When the need for radio silence is over, the station in control of the distress traffic can open the channel for routine communications by announcing "Seelonce Feenee."

"All ships,
all ships,
all ships,
this is
Brixham Coastguard,
Brixham Coastguard,
Brixham Coastguard,
Seelonce Feenee,
Out."

Mayday Relay

Syllabus item D1.1

There are, unfortunately, plenty of reasons why a Mayday may not reach the Search and Rescue authorities.

It may be that the vessel concerned has been dismasted, and is having to use an emergency antenna (or no antenna at all).

It may be that the battery is being lapped by rising bilge water, so the power available is low.

It may be that the message is being sent from a hand-held radio because the vessel's main radio is surrounded by smoke and flames

or it may just be that it is out of radio range.

Whatever the reason, if you hear a Distress message but do not hear an acknowledgement or further radio traffic from the casualty that suggests her call has been acknowledged, you may be able to assist by acting as a relay station. The proword "Mayday Relay" makes it clear that you are not in distress yourself, but are passing on a message for someone else.

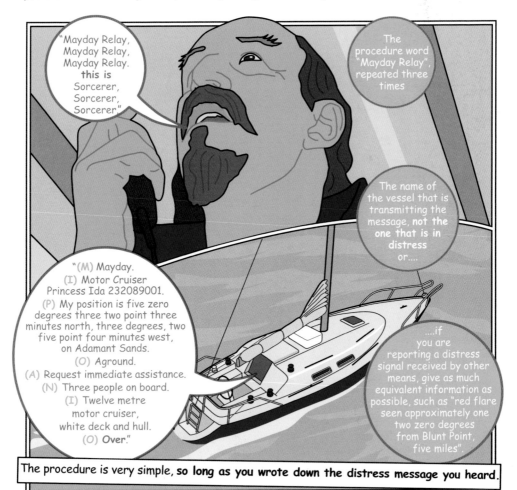

The procedure is very simple, so long as you wrote down the distress message you heard.

Voice procedure 3: Urgency & Safety calls

Urgency calls

Syllabus items D1.2 and C2.2

It is easy to think of situations in which a Mayday call would not be justified, but which still warrant some kind of special treatment. The drifting motor boat example on page 43 is just one example that justifies the use of an Urgency Call, using the proword "Panpan" (from the French "panne", meaning "breakdown") to claim priority over all other calls except Distress communications.

The official definition of an urgency situation is "when the calling station has a very urgent message to transmit concerning the safety of a ship, aircraft or other vehicle, or the safety of a person."

Unlike a Mayday or Mayday Relay, a Panpan call is not a broadcast: it should be addressed to someone — even though, in many cases, that "someone" will be "All ships".

An urgency call should always be made on Channel 16, using High Power.

Panpan,
Panpan,
Panpan.
All ships,
all ships,
all ships,
this is
Snow White,
Snow White,
Snow White,

Immediately following the urgency call, without waiting for a reply, send the urgency message. There is no rigid format for an urgency message, but in most cases, the "PDANIO" section of a distress message is a good template:-

P	Position	Two six zero degrees from Longships light, nine miles
D	Distress	Adrift in the traffic separation scheme
A	Assistance	Request a tow
N	Number	Three persons on board
I	Information	A twelve metre motor cruiser
O	Over	

Medical advice

Syllabus item D1.2

One special case of an Urgency Call deals with situations in which you are asking for medical advice.

> It involves a Panpan call, but addressed to the Coastguard, rather than to All Ships. The associated message can be reduced to "request medical advice":-

> "Panpan,
> Panpan,
> Panpan.
> Clyde Coastguard,
> Clyde Coastguard,
> Clyde Coastguard,
> **this is**
> Sheherazade,
> Sheherazade,
> Sheherazade,
> Request urgent medical advice
> Over."

What happens next is largely in the hands of the Coastguard. Around the UK, you can expect to be asked to transfer to a duplex working channel, such as 23, 84, or 86, where you will be linked to a hospital doctor who has been specially trained to give advice by radio to casualties at sea. While the call is being connected, the Coastguard is also likely to ask for more information about the vessel and its position, in case the request for advice escalates into a need for a helicopter or lifeboat.

The proword "Panpan Medico", referred to in some old reference books, is no longer used. The proword "Medical" is still used, but only in the context of medical transports in war.

Safety calls

Safety calls and messages are identified by the proword "Securitay", pronounced as the French word "sécurité", meaning "safety", and relate to gale and navigational warnings. Although ships and small craft are not prohibited from transmitting safety calls, they are more likely to be on the receiving end of a call from a coast radio station such as a Coastguard or Harbourmaster.

Although safety calls are made on Channel 16, they are not of such high priority as Distress or Urgency messages, so the safety message itself is passed on a working channel.

GMDSS

Background and principles

Throughout most of the last century, the radio equipment ships were required to carry was based on their size and the number of passengers they carried. So a cross-channel ferry — quite a large vessel, carrying lots of passengers — was required to carry equipment capable of world-wide communications, and a fully-qualified radio officer to operate it, despite the fact that it was never much more than ten miles from port.

A small tramp steamer, on the other hand, could set off across the Pacific with an MF radio which would struggle to reach two hundred miles. If it had to send a distress message, it was largely a matter of luck whether there would be anyone within range or not.

In 1979, the International Maritime Organisation decided that modern technology could do better, and that a **Global Maritime Distress and Safety System (GMDSS)** was called for. New regulations came into force in 1992, phasing-in the system over a period of seven years.

The main idea was that all ships should carry at least two independent means of transmitting distress alerts directly to search and rescue authorities ashore. To this were added a number of supplementary requirements, including a means of communicating with other vessels nearby, and of receiving navigational and weather warnings.

To decide what equipment is required for any particular vessel, the world is divided into four areas.

A1 areas are within VHF coverage of a suitably-equipped Search and Rescue centre

A2 areas are within MF coverage of a suitably-equipped Search and Rescue centre

A3 areas are within Inmarsat satellite communication coverage

A4 areas are beyond the coverage of Inmarsat satellite communication — i.e. within about 1200 miles of the north or south pole.

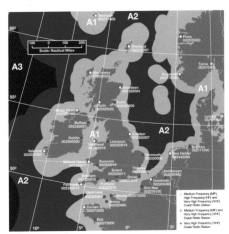

A larger version of this chart is shown on pages 84-85

Sub-systems involved in GMDSS

The Global Maritime Distress and Safety System is not really a communication system: it's a legal framework of equipment requirements and operating procedures, involving several different communication systems. Some of these, such as HF, MF, and VHF radio, existed before GMDSS was thought of: others were developed in the twenty years that elapsed between the decision to implement GMDSS, and the 1999 deadline for its full operation.

Navtex

Syllabus item C4

"Navtex" is an abbreviation for Navigation Teletext. It delivers written navigational warnings and weather forecasts to vessels within a few hundred miles of most of the world's coastlines.

Navtex transmitters are dotted around the world coastlines, typically a couple of hundred miles apart, but all transmitting on one of two frequencies: 518kHz or 490MHz. Operating at the lower end of the MF band (see page 9) means that each transmitter has a range of several hundred miles, but they don't interfere with each other because they are divided into groups, in which each transmitter has its own twenty minute "slot" once every four hours.

When its turn comes, each transmitter broadcasts all the messages it has on hand, giving each one a "header" that identifies where it has come from, what subject it covers (weather, navigation, ice etc.,) and a serial number.

Dedicated Navtex receivers can decode the messages, either printing them out on paper, or displaying them on a screen.

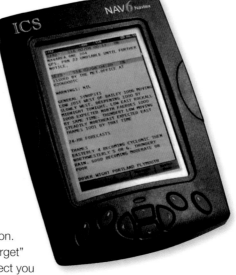

The receiver can be programmed to ignore certain types of massage, or to ignore messages from certain stations. If you are cruising the Irish Sea, for instance, you probably don't want weather forecasts for Portugal or ice warnings for northern Norway.

It will also ignore repetitions of messages which it has already recieved.

• If possible, leave your Navtex receiver switched on. If you switch it on and off during a cruise, it will "forget" which messages it has already received, and subject you to numerous repetitions.

One of the best features of Navtex, for British users, is that all transmissions on the "standard" Navtex service (518kHz) everywhere in the world, are in English. The other frequency (490kHz) is used for a "local" Navtex service. Some countries use this to provide a service in their own language, but in the UK it is used for supplementary information, such as the Inshore Waters weather forecast.

EPIRBs

Emergency Position Indicating Radio Beacons (EPIRBs) are fundamental to the GMDSS. For vessels which are legally required to conform to GMDSS, they provide one of the two "independent means" of communicating with SAR authorities. For "voluntary fit" vessels, including pleasure craft and small commercial craft operating under MCGA Codes of Practice, they are a very cost-effective means of providing distress alerting with world-wide coverage.

Unfortunately the term EPIRB is used to describe several different quite different types of equipment. In this book, and in the context of GMDSS, the term "EPIRB" refers to a 406MHz EPIRB.

Some EPIRBs are capable of indicating their position, but most are not. Their main purpose is to transmit a distress alert, coded to show the identity of the vessel concerned, which can be detected by satellites of the Cospas-Sarsat system. The satellites use doppler positioning (see page 58) to calculate where the signal is coming from, and then download the details of the EPIRB's identity and position to receiving stations ashore.

Direction finding equipment can't be used on the 406MHz EPIRB signal, so, to allow rescue vessels and aircraft to home in on a casualty, all 406MHz EPIRBs also transmit a homing signal on the lower frequency of 121.5MHz.

For very short range direction finding, they also have a bright flashing light.

The satellites

The **Cospas-Sarsat** system is an astonishing international venture that was set up in 1979, by the Soviet Union, USA, Canada, and France. It uses at least four (usually more) satellites in low polar orbits, less than 1000km above the Earth's surface. Because they are so low, they have to fly fast to resist the pull of gravity, so each satellite goes round the earth about 14 times per day. As the Earth revolves inside the satellite orbits, the result is that each satellite passes over a different part of the Earth's surface each time it goes round.

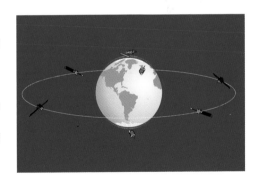

They are supplemented by three **Geosar** satellites. These go round the Earth almost 36,000km above the equator, where they take precisely 24 hours to complete one orbit. The result is that each satellite "hovers" over a fixed position on the Earth's surface.

The two systems complement each other:-

Cospas-Sarsat satellites can work out the position of a standard 406MHz EPIRB, but may not be able to download it to an earth station until they happen to pass over one.
Geosar satellites cannot work out the position of an EPIRB unless the signal includes position information, but can download the distress alert, identity, and position to an earth station immediately.

Doppler positioning

In everyday life, the "Doppler effect" is probably most noticeable when you're standing by the side of a busy road: it makes the sound of each car change in pitch at the moment it passes you. The same thing happens to the EPIRB transmissions as they are received by a satellite: when the satellite is flying towards the EPIRB, it receives a slightly higher frequency than when it is flying

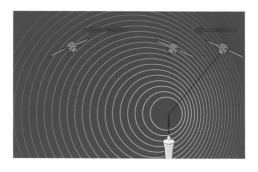

away from it. Only at the instant at which the satellite is closest to the EPIRB does it receive a signal at the exact frequency that was transmitted. By analysing how quickly the frequency changes, the satellite can also work out how far from the EPIRB it passed.

EPIRBs

EPIRBs vary in their design and operation, but can be divided into two groups:-

Category 1 EPIRBs are stowed in brackets from which they are released and activated automatically if immersed to a depth of 2-4 metres.

Category 2 EPIRBs have to be manually removed from their brackets. Depending on the make and model, they may be activated by turning the right way up, by dropping into sea water, or by a manual switch.

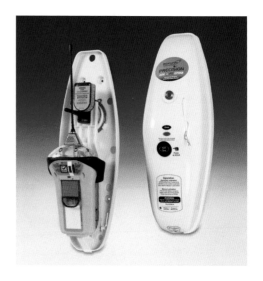

Stowage and maintenance

Category 1 EPIRBs must always be stowed in their brackets, mounted somewhere on the upper deck of the vessel, where they can be relied upon to float free if the vessel sinks.

Category 2 EPIRBs can be stowed anywhere where they can easily be reached in a distress situation.

> Both types should be tested regularly, at least once a season, in accordance with the manufacturer's instructions.
>
> The battery must be replaced in accordance with the manufacturer's instructions, usually once every five years.
>
> The release mechanism must be checked to ensure that the EPIRB can be manually released, on a regular basis, and hydrostatic release mechanisms should be serviced or replaced every two years.
>
> Under no circumstances should an EPIRB be triggered to send a distress alert during testing or maintenance.

Registration

Every EPIRB has its own unique identity code, which is transmitted as part of its distress alert. It is obviously important for the search and rescue authorities to know which vessel the code relates to, so the EPIRB has to be registered with the SAR authorities in the country in which the vessel is registered.

Although the existence of an EPIRB on board should be included in your application for a ship radio licence, this does not, in itself, constitute registration. In the UK, separate EPIRB registration forms are available from the EPIRB registry, at Falmouth Coastguard, and should be returned to them.

False Alarms

The automatic operation of EPIRBs makes them particularly prone to generating false alarms. These should be minimised by making sure that the EPIRB is switched off when the vessel is not in use, and by wrapping it in two layers of kitchen foil whenever it has to be transported.

> If an EPIRB is accidentally triggered, do not switch it off. Contact the nearest Search and Rescue authority (the Coastguard, in UK waters) by any means available to you. Explain what has happened, and wait to be told to switch the EPIRB off.

SARTs

Syllabus item C5.3

The initials SART stand for Search And Rescue Transponder, and refer to a device operating on radar frequencies, designed to produce a distinctive pattern on an approaching vessel's radar.

A marine radar works by transmitting short pulses of super high frequency radio waves, which are focused into a tight beam by a directional antenna. When a pulse meets a "target", such as a ship, it is reflected back to the radar. The time between transmission of the pulse and reception of the echo is directly related to the distance between the radar and the target. Of course, this only happens when the directional antenna is pointing at the target, so the direction the antenna is pointing corresponds to the direction of the target.

The range and bearing information is then used to "paint" a blob (called a "contact") on the radar display, in a position corresponding to the target's range and bearing.

A SART, however, does not merely reflect the radar pulse: it transmits a sequence of twelve pulses at very short intervals. On the radar screen, this appears as a string of twelve small contacts, starting at the position of the SART, and stretching outwards towards the edge of the screen, 0.6 miles apart.

As the vessel closes to within about a mile of the SART, the twelve contacts expand to wide arcs, and when the vessel reaches the SART, the arcs may expand even further, to form a pattern of twelve concentric circles.

The performance of a SART varies: although it should be visible to a ship's radar at five miles or more, this reduces to less than two miles if the SART is lying on the floor of a liferaft, but can be as much as forty miles.

SARTs are primarily intended for use in liferafts, but can be used on any vessel

A SART should generally be mounted as high as possible, and at least 1m above sea level

Do not use a radar reflector and SART together

Digital Selective Calling is a facility which automates many of the procedures which would otherwise be carried out by voice on Channel 16.

It's an important part of GMDSS because it allows distress alerts to be transmitted simply by pressing a button, but this is not its only purpose: DSC can also speed up and simplify routine calls, so long as both vessels have the right equipment.

DSC Controllers

Syllabus items B2.1 and B2.5

"The right equipment" means a DSC controller, which may either be built into a radio, or added as a separate component.

All radios sold since April 2000 have been required either to have a DSC controller built in, or to be capable of being connected to a DSC controller.

On vessels which are not required by law to carry VHF, it is still legitimate to continue to use an older radio without DSC, or to install and use a new radio without its associated DSC controller.

A DSC controller works by creating a coded message. It's a bit like morse code, except that instead of dots and dashes it uses ones and zeros; and instead of a flashing light it uses musical notes. If you could hear the message, it would sound like a high-pitched warble, but at 1200 notes per second, it is far too fast for any human ear to pick out individual tones.

The digital message can include several different types of information. In the case of a routine ship-to-ship call, for instance, it would include:-

      A "format specifier" identifying the type of call
      A nine-digit number identifying the vessel being called
      A similar nine-digit number identifying the vessel that is calling
      A suggested working channel

This burst of data, lasting about half a second, is passed from the DSC controller to the radio, which transmits it on Channel 70 (see page 29).

Any vessel with DSC that is within range will receive the call, but in most cases, nothing will happen.

On the vessel that is being called, however, the DSC controller will recognise its unique identification number, and sound an alarm to draw attention to the fact that it is being called. At the same time, it will display the identity of the calling vessel on its screen.

Assuming the operator decides to accept the call, he can acknowledge it — usually by pressing a button on his own DSC controller. This switches his radio to the appropriate working channel, and sends another burst of digital data back to the original caller, signalling that the call has been acknowledged, and switching the radio to the chosen working channel, ready for normal voice traffic.

Classes of DSC Controller

There are several classes of DSC controller, with different capabilities to suit the needs of different users.

Class A controllers offer all the facilities available from DSC, including the ability to control HF and MF radios, to acknowledge or relay distress messages, and to make calls to vessels within a chosen geographical area. They are intended primarily for commercial vessels, and are seldom installed in small craft.

Class B controllers are also intended primarily for commercial vessels, but offer a reduced DSC capability. They comply with the minimum requirements for vessels which are required by law to carry MF and VHF radio, but cannot control HF radios, or make geographical area calls.

Class D controllers are intended primarily for small craft. They offer a reduced DSC capability, for VHF only, but do not conform to all the requirements for vessels which are required by law to carry VHF radio (other than small commercial craft operating under MCA Codes of Practice).

Class E controllers are also intended primarily for small craft, and offer a reduced DSC capability, for MF and HF only, and do not conform to all the requirements for vessels which are required by law to carry VHF radio.

MMSIs

Syllabus item B2.3

DSC cannot handle boat names, any more than an automatic telephone exchange can handle names or addresses. Instead, every vessel with a DSC controller is issued with a unique nine-digit number, known as its Maritime Mobile Service Identity (MMSI).

In the UK, MMSIs are issued by Ofcom when they are requested to do so by ticking a box on the application form or renewal form for a Ship Radio Licence.

The first three digits of a ship's MMSI are known as the Maritime Identification Digits (MID), and indicate the country which issued it.

All UK vessels have MMSIs which begin with the numbers 232; 233; 234; or 235 eg. 232089001

Coast radio stations also have nine-digit MMSIs, but to distinguish them from ships and boats, their MMSIs always begin with two zeros. This is followed by the three-digit MID, then by four more digits

eg Milford Haven Coastguard 002320017

DSC can also handle **group calls**, to a group of vessels which share some common interest, such as all vessels belonging to one company, or all the yachts taking part in a race. The Group MMSI is allocated by Ofcom on request, and consists of a single zero, followed by the MID, then by five more digits

eg 023208591

A DSC controller must have its MMSI stored in its memory before it can be used. Most Class D controllers allow individual owners to do this themselves... but only once. If you make a mistake, or if you move the controller onto a boat with a different MMSI, the controller will have to be returned to its supplier to have its memory erased.

Group MMSIs, however, are different: these can be saved and deleted as often as you like.

Types of call

Syllabus items B2.2 and B2.4

The DSC code allows calls to be classified into six different types:

Distress
All ships
Individual — a call to a specific vessel or coast station
Geographic area — to all stations within a designated area (not on class D controllers)
Group call — to all stations sharing a "common interest" and with the same Group MMSI
Automatic or semi-automatic service call through a coast radio station to a public telephone system (not on class D controllers)

These tell the DSC controller at the receiving end what will be in the rest of the DSC message, and how it should react: it may sound an audible alarm for an incoming distress message, for instance, that is quite different from the alarm sound associated with a routine ship-to-ship call.

The coded DSC transmission also includes an indication of a call's priority:-

Distress — equivalent to "Mayday" in voice procedure
Urgency — equivalent to "Panpan" in voice procedure
Safety — equivalent to "Securitay" in voice procedure
Ship's business (not on class D controllers)
Routine

In most cases, the priority of the call is decided automatically by the software within the DSC controller. It is pretty obvious, for instance, that a distress call cannot be sent with anything less than distress priority.

DSC controllers and position

A DSC controller needs to "know" the boat's position, if only so that it can include it in a distress alert.

To do this, it must be interfaced (connected) to a GPS receiver, which will then send position and time updates to the DSC controller about once every second or so.

As a back-up, the position and time can be keyed in manually.

Using a Class D controller

Syllabus item B2.6

There is no standard layout for the control panel of a Class D DSC controller, although there are certain similarities between the different makes and models:-

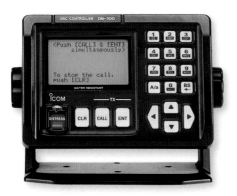

they all feature a prominent "Distress" button, protected by a cover to prevent accidental operation

most have an alphanumeric keypad, similar to that of a mobile phone

Other controls are used for selecting items from a "menu" of functions: these
may include:-

> dedicated, one-job buttons
> up, down, "clear", and "enter" keys
> "soft" keys, whose purpose changes depending on the task in hand, but whose current
> label always appears on the screen.

Sending a DSC call

There are corresponding differences and similarities in the sequence of operations required to
compose a DSC message. A typical sequence is something like this:-

1. Press <Call> to show the DSC menu on the screen
2. Select the type of call from the options available (Individual; Group; All ships; Distress)
    - Press <Enter> to confirm your selection, and reveal the next menu
3. For an individual call, either:-
    select "Manual entry" and type in the other station's MMSI number
    or
    select the name of the station you want to contact from the "phone book" stored in the
    unit's memory
    - Press <Enter> to confirm your selection, and reveal the next menu
4. Select a working channel
    - Press <Enter> to confirm your selection, and reveal the next menu
5. Press <Call> and <Enter> together to transmit the DSC call.

> This is only one example, based on the procedure for the Icom DS100 DSC
> controller. Other makes and models are different: On Simrad's DSC 1400, for
> instance, you must not press the <Enter> key to confirm each step, because
> pressing it tells the controller that the whole message is complete, and that you
> would like it to be sent immediately!

Receiving a DSC individual call

When a DSC controller recognises its own MMSI in an incoming DSC call, it sounds an alarm,
similar to the ringtone of a telephone.

To answer it, on most controllers, is a simple matter of pressing a single key. On the Icom
DS 100, for instance, it is the "enter" key: on the Simrad RT1400, it is one of four "soft" keys
indicated by an on-screen label representing a telephone handset.

This prompts the DSC controller to transmit an acknowledgement and, at the same time, to
switch its own radio to the working channel that was suggested.

Receiving a DSC group call

A DSC controller that has been programmed with a Group MMSI will respond to calls addressed to the Group MMSI as well as to individual calls addressed to its own MMSI.

The alarm sound may be different, but a more significant point is that "acknowledging" a Group call will only mute the alarm and switch your receiver to the specified working channel: it will not send an acknowledgement to the calling vessel.

Using a Class A or B controller

Syllabus item B2.6

If an SRC operator finds himself using a Class A or B controller, it is important to bear in mind that the equipment is capable of carrying out some operations that have been deliberately removed from the options available on a Class D controller.

In particular, you should **NOT**:-

Use DSC to relay distress messages (use the Mayday Relay procedure on page 51 instead)

Use DSC to acknowledge distress messages (use voice procedure on page 49 instead)

No two makes or models are identical...

... so read the manual

Definition of distress

The definition of distress, for DSC purposes, is exactly the same as its definition for voice procedure:-

> A distress situation is one in which:-
> a vessel, vehicle, aircraft or person
> is in
> grave and imminent danger.

The Distress alert

Syllabus item C2.1

A vital feature of every DSC controller is the distress button which, when pressed, prompts the equipment to compose a distress alert, including the vessel's MMSI and its current position. The alert is then passed to the radio to be transmitted — like all DSC messages — on Channel 70.

Unlike an individual DSC call (see page 65), a DSC distress alert is automatically addressed to "all stations", so it triggers an alarm on every DSC controller within range.

Such a highly automated system makes it easy to send distress alerts, but it also has the potential for generating huge numbers of false alerts, either by mistake or by malice. There isn't much that can be done about hoax calls, but to minimise accidental false alarms, the rules say that the Distress button must be protected by a cover, and must not trigger a distress alert unless it is held down for several seconds — usually five seconds.

Unless the situation is so desperate that every second counts, it is well worth refining the basic Distress alert to give an indication of the nature of distress.

As with a routine call, the sequence of operations for achieving this varies between different makes and models: it may, for instance, be achieved through the "Call" menu, or through a special menu which reveals itself when the Distress button is pressed and released.

In either case, you will be presented with a number of options, from which you select the most appropriate:-

Undesignated
(the default option,
included in the basic
distress alert)

Fire or explosion

Flooding

Collision

Grounding

Listing (or in danger of capsizing)

Sinking

Disabled and adrift

Abandoning ship

Piracy

Man overboard

You may have to press the <Enter> key to confirm your selection, but in any case you will have to press and hold the Distress button for several seconds in order to send the Distress Alert.

- Read the manual
- Practise composing distress alerts

but

- **Never** send a distress alert unless you are really in distress

After sending a Distress alert Syllabus item C2.1

The whole point of GMDSS is that vessels at sea no longer have to rely on luck for their distress alert to be heard: assuming they have the right equipment for their area of operations, there is a very good chance that their distress alert will be received by the Search and Rescue authorities ashore.

- In case it is not, however, all DSC controllers are programmed to automatically repeat the distress alert at random intervals of approximately four minutes until it is either acknowledged or switched off.

A DSC Distress alert does not contain as much information as a Mayday call by voice, nor can it be received by vessels without DSC — some of whom might be very well placed to assist.

> A DSC alert should always be immediately followed by a Mayday call and message, transmitted by voice on Channel 16 (see page 44), with the MMSI number included as part of the vessel's identity.

Receiving a distress alert Syllabus item C2.1

In many respects, a DSC Distress alert is very much like a Mayday message sent by voice, in that anyone receiving it is obliged to accept it, and to offer assistance if they can. Just like a Mayday message, however, that principle needs to be diluted with common sense:-

> if it is likely that a coast radio station (such as the coastguard) will have received the message, allow time for them to respond before doing so yourself
>
> if you are not in a position to offer effective assistance, do not respond
>
> if you are able to assist, and have not heard anything from the coastguard within a few minutes, acknowledge the alert by voice on Channel 16, using the procedure on page 48
>
> unless you are acknowledging and assisting, maintain radio silence on any channel being used for distress communications.

Acknowledging a DSC distress alert by DSC automatically prevents further repetitions, so

- Class D DSC controllers **cannot** acknowledge or relay a DSC Distress alert
- Class A or B DSC controllers **should not** be used to acknowledge or relay a DSC Distress alert except on specific instructions from the Search and Rescue authorities.

Accidental False Alert procedure

Syllabus items C3.1; C3.6

If you are unlucky enough to find that you have somehow managed to transmit an accidental false distress alert, the first thing to do is not to repeat it!

Urgency and Safety

Syllabus item C2.2

DSC can also be used in situations which do not warrant a full-blown distress alert, to draw attention to Panpan or Securitay messages.

A DSC **urgency** call is equivalent to the proword Panpan: it means "I have a very urgent message to transmit concerning the safety of a mobile unit or person".

A DSC **safety** call is equivalent to the proword Securitay: it means "I have an important navigational or meteorological warning to transmit".

> Unlike a DSC distress alert, a DSC urgency or safety call contains no information other than the MMSI of the station transmitting it and the working channel that will be used for a subsequent voice message, so it must always be followed up immediately by a Panpan or Securitay message by voice.

Sending an urgency or safety call

There are no dedicated "urgency" or "safety" buttons on a DSC controller, so the procedure for sending an urgency or safety call is, in some respects, more like that required to send a routine call. Just as for a routine call, the exact sequence of buttons to press varies from make to make and model to model, but a typical sequence is something like this:-

1. Press <Call> to show the DSC menu on the screen
2. Select "All ships" from the list of available call types (Individual; Group; All ships; Distress)
    - Press <Enter> to confirm your selection, and reveal the next menu
3. Select "Urgency" or "Safety"
    - Press <Enter> to confirm your selection, and reveal the next menu
4. Select a working channel (usually Channel 16)
5. Press <Call> and <Enter> together to transmit the DSC call
6. Follow up with a voice call and message using the Panpan or Securitay procedure (see pages 52-54)

This is included as an example only, but is based on the procedure for the Class D Icom DS100 DSC controller. Other makes and models are different:-

On the Class D Simrad DSC 1400, for instance, the call types offered are Routine, Safety, Urgency and Group. Having selected Urgency or Group, there are no more options: pressing the <Enter> key immediately sends the call to all ships with Channel 16 as the working channel.

Class A or B controllers offer the option of addressing urgency or safety calls to individual ships or coast radio stations. This feature is deliberately not made available on Class D controllers, to keep them as easy to use as possible.

> No two makes or models are identical...so read the manual!

Receiving a DSC urgency or safety call

"Acknowledging" an urgency or safety call that was sent to all ships will mute the alarm and switch your receiver to the specified working channel: it will not send an acknowledgement to the calling vessel.

Mayday relay

One of the problems of DSC is that it is so highly automated that sending distress messages has become almost too easy: it is now possible to send a distress alert without meaning to. To prevent these accidental distress alerts being multiplied by well-meaning radio operators relaying them, Class D controllers are incapable of relaying DSC distress alerts, and operators of Class A or B controllers are not allowed to use their DSC Mayday Relay facility except under exceptional circumstances.

> If you receive a DSC Distress alert that has not been acknowledged within five minutes, you should attempt to contact the casualty by voice on Channel 16, and inform the nearest coastguard — also by voice, on Channel 16.

This does not, however, prevent you from relaying a Mayday message that was received by voice. If you have not heard an acknowledgement to a voice Mayday within a minute or so, and there is no radio traffic suggesting that she is in contact with potential rescuers, you should send a DSC Urgency alert, immediately followed by a Mayday Relay message using the voice procedure on page 51.

Appendix 1: Examination Syllabus for the CEPT Short Range Certificate (SRC)

A. General Knowledge of VHF Radiotelephone communications in the Maritime Mobile Service.

A1. The general principles and basic features of the maritime mobile service relevant to vessels not subject to a compulsory fit under the SOLAS Convention

1.1 Types of communication in the maritime mobile service
 Distress, urgency and safety communications
 Public correspondence
 Port operations service
 Ship movement service
 Intership communication
 On board communications

1.2 Types of station in the maritime mobile service
 Ship stations
 Coast stations
 Pilot stations, port stations etc.
 Aircraft stations
 Rescue Coordination Centre (RCC)

1.3 Elementary knowledge of radio frequencies and channels appropriate to the VHF maritime mobile band
 The concept of frequency
 Propagation on VHF frequencies
 Range for voice communications
 Range for DSC transmissions
 The usage of VHF frequencies in the maritime mobile service
 The concept of radio channel: simplex, semi-duplex and duplex
 Channel plan for VHF, including allocations for the GMDSS
 Distress and safety channels
 National channels for small craft safety
 Intership communications
 Port operations
 Ship movement
 Calling channels
 Public correspondence channels

1.4 Functionality of ship station equipment
 Sources of energy of ship stations
 Batteries
 Different kinds of batteries and their characteristics
 Charging
 Maintenance of batteries

B. Detailed working knowledge of radio equipment

B1. The VHF radio installation

1.1   Radiotelephone channels
> Channel selection and controls
> Dual watch facilities and controls

1.2   Basic controls and usage, e.g.
> Connecting the power
> Press to transmit switch
> High/low output power switch
> Volume control
> Squelch control
> Dimmer

1.3   Portable two-way VHF radiotelephone apparatus

1.4   Maritime VHF antennas

B2. Purpose and use of Digital Selective Calling (DSC) facilities

2.1   The general principles and basic features of DSC
> DSC messages
> DSC attempt
> Call acknowledgement
> Call relay

2.2   Types of call
> Distress call
> All ships call
> Call to individual station
> Geographic area call
> Group call

2.3   The Maritime Mobile Service Identity (MMSI) number system
> The nationality identification: Maritime Identification Digits (MID)
> Ship station numbers
> Coast station numbers

2.4   Call categorisation and priority
> Distress
> Urgency
> Safety
> Ship business
> Routine

C. Operational procedures of the GMDSS and detailed practical operation of GMDSS subsystems and equipment.

C1. Search and Rescue (SAR) Procedures in the GMDSS

C2. Distress, urgency and safety communication procedures in the GMDSS

5.3   Search and Rescue Radar Transponder (SART)
            Operation
            Operating height
            Effect of radar reflector
            Range of a SART transmitter

D. Operational Procedures and regulations for VHF Radiotelephone communications

D1. Ability to exchange communications relevant to the safety of life at sea

1.1   Distress communications
            Distress signal
            The correct use and meaning of the signal MAYDAY
            Distress call
            Distress message
            Acknowledgement of a distress message
            Obligation to acknowledge a distress message
            Correct form of acknowledgement
            Action to be taken following acknowledgement
            The control of distress traffic
            The correct use and meanings of the signals:
                SEELONCE MAYDAY
                SEELONCE FEENEE
        Transmission of a distress message by a station not itself in distress
        The correct use and meaning of the signal MAYDAY RELAY

1.2   Urgency communications
            Urgency signal
            The correct use and meaning of the signal PAN-PAN
            Urgency message
            Obtaining urgent medical advice through a Coast Station

1.3   Safety communications
            Safety signal
            The correct use and meaning of the signal SECURITE
            Safety message
            Special procedures for communication with appropriate national
            organisations on matters affecting safety

1.4   Reception of MSI by VHF radiotelephony

1.5　　Awareness of the existence and use of the IMO Standard Marine Navigational Vocabulary
> Knowledge of the following basic signals:-
>> ALL AFTER; ALL BEFORE; CORRECT; CORRECTION;
>> IN FIGURES; IN LETTERS; I SAY AGAIN; I SPELL;
>> OUT; OVER; RADIO CHECK; READ BACK; RECEIVED;
>> SAY AGAIN; STATION CALLING; TEXT; TRAFFIC; THIS IS; WAIT;
>> WORD AFTER; WORD BEFORE; WRONG

1.6　　Use of international phonetic alphabet

D2. Regulations, obligatory procedures and practices

2.1　　Awareness of international documentation and availability of national publications

2.2　　Knowledge of the international regulations and agreements governing the maritime mobile service
> Requirement for Ship Station Licence
> Regulations concerning control of the operation of radio equipment by the holder of an appropriate certificate of competence
> National regulations concerning the radio record keeping
> Preservation of the secrecy of correspondence
> Types of call and types of message which are prohibited

D3. Practical and theoretical knowledge of radiotelephone procedures

3.1　　Public correspondence and radiotelephone call procedures
> Method of calling a Coast Station by radiotelephony
> Ordering for a manually switched link call
> Ending the call
> Calls to ships from Coast Stations
> Special facilities of calls
> Method of calling a coast station by DSC for general communications
> Selecting an automatic radiotelephone call

3.2　　Traffic charges
> International charging system
> Accounting Authority Identification Code (AAIC)

3.3　　Practical traffic routines
> Correct use of callsigns
> Procedure for establishing communication on intership, public correspondence, small craft safety and port operation and ship movement channels
> Procedure for unanswered calls and garbled calls
> Control of communications

Appendix 2: Standard Marine Navigational Vocabulary

1 Procedure/message markers

When it is necessary to indicate that phrases in this vocabulary are to be used, the following messages may be sent:

"Please use the Standard Marine Navigational Vocabulary."
"I will use the Standard Marine Navigational Vocabulary."

If necessary, external communication messages may be preceded by the following message markers:

QUESTION indicates that the following message is of interrogative character

ANSWER indicates that the following message is the reply to a previous question

REQUEST indicates that the contents of the following message are asking for action from others with respect to the ship

INFORMATION indicates that the following message is restricted to observed facts

INTENTION indicates that the following message informs others about immediate navigational actions intended to be taken

WARNING indicates that the following message informs other traffic participants about dangers

ADVICE indicates that the following message implies the intention of the sender to influence the recipient(s) by a recommendation

INSTRUCTION indicates that the following message implies the intention of the sender to influence the recipient(s) by a regulation.

2 Standard verbs

Where possible, sentences should be introduced by one of the following verb forms:

IMPERATIVE: Always to be used when mandatory orders are being given	INDICATIVE	NEGATIVE	INTERROGATIVE
You must	I require	I do not require	Do I require?
Do not	I am / You are	I am not / You are not	Am I? / Are you?
Must I?	I have	I do not have	Do you have?
	I can	I cannot	Can I?
	I wish to	I do not wish	Can you?
	I will	I will not	Do you wish to?
	You may	You need not	May I?
	Advise	Advise not	Is there?
	There is	There is not	Where is/are?
			When is/are?

3 Responses

Where the answer to a question is in the affirmative, say:

"yes . . ." — followed by the appropriate phrase in full.

Where the answer to a question is in the negative, say:

"no . . . " — followed by the appropriate phrase in full.

Where the information is not immediately available but soon will be, say:

"Stand by".

Where the information cannot be obtained, say:

"No information".

Where a message is not properly heard, say:

"Say again".

Where a message is not understood, say:

"Message not understood".

4 Distress/urgency/safety messages

MAYDAY (repeated three times) is to be used to announce a distress message

PAN PAN (repeated three times) is to be used to announce an urgency message

SECURITE (repeated three times) is to be used to announce a safety message

5 Miscellaneous phrases

What is your name (and call sign)?

How do you read me?

I read you . . .

bad/1

poor/2

fair/3

good/4

excellent/5

with signal strength . . .

1/barely perceptible

2/weak

3/fairly good

4/good

5/very good

Stand by on channel . . .

Change to channel . . .

I cannot read you.

I cannot understand you.

Please use the . . .

        Standard Marine Navigational Vocabulary

        International Code of Signals

I am passing a message for vessel . . .

Correction . . .

I am ready to receive your message.

I am not ready to receive your message.

I do not have channel . . . Please use channel . . .

6 Repetition

If any parts of the message are considered sufficiently important to need safeguarding, use the word "repeat".

> *Examples:* "You will load 163 repeat 163 tons bunkers."
> "Do not repeat not overtake."

7 Position

When latitude and longitude are used, these shall be expressed in degrees arid minutes (and decimals of a minute if necessary), north or south of the Equator and east or west of Greenwich.

When the position is related to a mark, the mark shall be a well-defined charted object. The bearing shall be in the 360 degree notation from true north and shall be that of the position FROM the mark.

> *Examples:* "There are salvage operations in position 15 degrees 34 minutes north 61 degrees 29 minutes west."
> "Your position is 137 degrees from Barr Head lighthouse distance two decimal four miles."

8 Courses

Always to be expressed in 360 degree notation from north (true north unless otherwise stated). Whether this is to TO or FROM a mark can be stated.

9 Bearings

The bearing of the mark or vessel concerned, is the bearing in the 360 degree notation from north (true north unless otherwise stated), except in the case of relative bearings. Bearings may be either FROM the mark or FROM the vessel.

> *Examples:* "The pilot boat is bearing 215° from you."
> "Your bearing is 127° from the signal station."

Note: Vessels reporting their position should always quote their bearing FROM the mark, as described in paragraph 7.

Relative bearings

Relative bearings can be expressed in degrees relative to the vessel's head or bow. More frequently this is in relation to the port or starboard bow.

> *Example:* "The buoy is 030° on your port bow."

Relative D/F bearings are more commonly expressed in the 360 degree notation.

10 Distances

Preferably to be expressed in nautical miles or cables (tenths of a mile) otherwise in kilometres or metres, the unit always to be stated.

11 Speed

To be expressed in knots:

(a) without further notation meaning speed through the water; or
(b) "ground speed" meaning speed over the ground.

12 Numbers

Numbers are to be spoken: "Onefive-zero" for 150.
"Two point five" for 2.5.

13 Geographical names

Place names used should be those on the chart or Sailing Directions in use. Should these not be understood, latitude and longitude should be given.

14 Time

Times should be expressed in the 24 hour notation indicating whether UTC, zone time or local shore time is being used.

Note: In cases not covered by the above phraseology normal radiotelephone practice will prevail.

Channel Selection Chart

Channel Designators		Transmitting frequencies (MHz)		Inter-ship	Port operations		Public Corresp.
		Ship stations	Coast stations		Single frequency	Two frequency	
	60	156.025	160.625			✓	✓
01		156.050	160.650			✓	✓
	61	156.075	160.675			✓	✓
02		156.100	160.700			✓	✓
	62	156.125	160.725			✓	✓
03		156.150	160.750			✓	✓
	63	156.175	160.775			✓	✓
04		156.200	160.800			✓	✓
	64	156.225	160.825			✓	✓
05		156.250	160.850			✓	✓
	65	156.275	160.875			✓	✓
06		156.300		✓			
	66	156.325	160.925			✓	✓
07		156.350	160.950			✓	✓
	67	156.375	156.375	✓	✓	HMCG SAR	
08		156.400		✓			
	68	156.425	156.425		✓		
09		156.450	156.450	✓	✓		
	69	156.475	156.475	✓	✓		
10		156.500	156.500	✓	✓	Oil Pollution	
	70	156.525	156.525		Digital selective calling for distress, safety and calling		
11		156.550	156.550		✓		
	71	156.575	156.575		✓		
12		156.600	156.600		✓		
	72	156.625		✓			
13		156.650	156.650	✓	✓		
	73	156.675	156.675	✓	✓	HMCG SAR	
14		156.700	156.700		✓		
	74	156.725	156.725		✓		

Channel Designators	Transmitting frequencies (MHz)		Inter-ship	Port operations		Public Corresp.
	Ship stations	Coast stations		Single frequency	Two frequency	
15	156.750	156.750	✓	✓	Also on-board coms	
75	156.775					
16	156.800	156.800		DISTRESS, SAFETY AND CALLING		
76	156.825			✓		
17	156.850	156.850	✓	✓	Also on-board coms	
77	156.875		✓			
18	156.900	161.500		✓	✓	✓
78	156.925	161.525			✓	✓
19	156.950	161.550			✓	✓
79	156.975	161.575			✓	✓
20	157.000	161.600			✓	✓
80	157.025	161.625	Also Marinas etc UK only		✓	✓
21	157.050	161.650			✓	✓
81	157.075	161.675			✓	✓
22	157.100	161.700			✓	✓
82	157.125	161.725	✓		✓	✓
23	157.150	161.750			HMCG SAR/MSI	
83	157.175	161.775	✓		✓	✓
24	157.200	161.800			✓	✓
84	157.225	161.825	✓		HMCG SAR/MSI	
25	157.250	161.850			✓	✓
85	157.275	161.875	✓		✓	✓
26	157.300	161.900			✓	✓
86	157.325	161.925	✓		HMCG SAR/MSI	
27	157.350	161.950			✓	✓
87	157.375			✓		
28	157.400	162.000			✓	✓
88	157.425			✓		
AIS 1	161.975	161.975				
AIS 2	162.025	162.025				

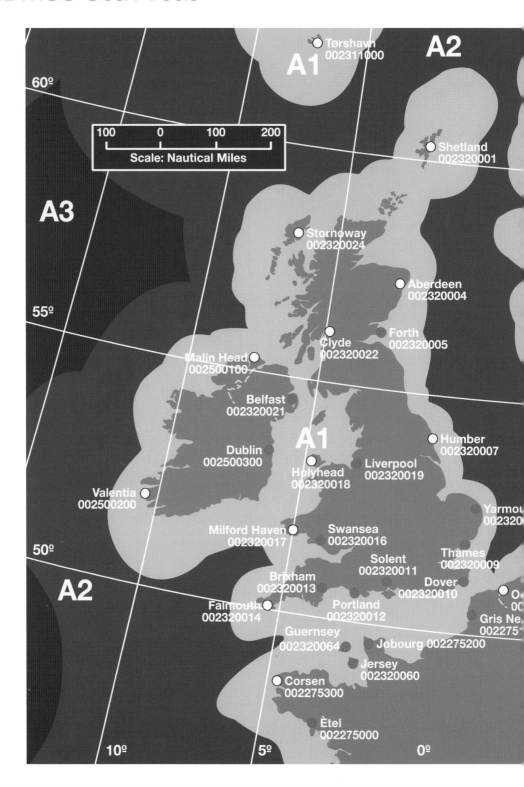

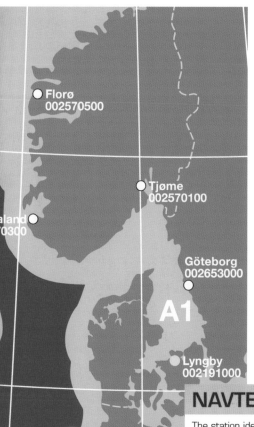

GMDSS Sea Areas

- Medium Frequency (MF),
  High Frequency (HF) and
  Very High Frequency (VHF)
  Coast Radio Station

- Medium Frequency (MF) and
  Very High Frequency (VHF)
  Coast Radio Station

- Very High Frequency (VHF)
  Coast Radio Station

Sea Area A1
The radiotelephone coverage of VHF coast
stations in which continuous alerting by
Digital Selective Calling (DSC) is available.

Sea Area A2
The radiotelephone coverage of MF coast
stations in which continuous alerting by
Digital Selective Calling is available.

Sea Area A3
The coverage of Inmarsat geostationary
satellites.

NAVTEX Sea Areas

The station identity letter allows the NAVTEX receiver to be
programmed to print out messages only for the desired service area.

L   International Service on 518kHz
U National Service on 490kHz

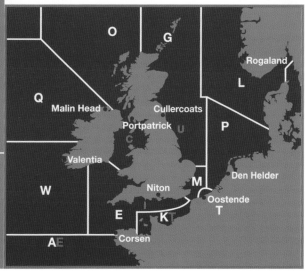

Index

Index

AM	Amplitude Modulation: superimposing an audio signal onto a radio wavel by varying the amplitude of the radio "carrier" wave
amplitude	the extent to which the voltage fluctuates in the electric field that makes up a radio wave, analogous to the "height" of a wave in water.
antenna	aerial
Authority to Operate	licence for a person to operate a VHF radio
broadcasting	transmitting a message without specifying who it is intended for
channel numbers	simple numerical identification of ITU standard frequencies
declaration of conformity	certification that radio conforms to performance standards
distress situation	vessel, vehicle, aircraft or person in grave and imminent danger
doppler positioning	using an apparent change in the frequency of the signal from a moving object to calculate position
DSC	Digital Selective Calling
Dual Watch	facility for radio to monitor Channel 16 and another channel concurrently
duplex channels	two-way, two-frequency operation
EPIRB	Emergency Position Indicating Radio Beacon
FM	Frequency Modulation: superimposing a audio signal onto a radio wave by varying the frequency of the radio "carrier".
frequency	speed of voltage changes in radio waves transmitted, in Hertz
gain	the factor by which an antenna increases effective radiated power or received signal strength, compared with a standard reference antenna
GMDSS	Global Maritime Distress and Safety System
guard band	restricted channels closest to Channel 16
IMO	International Maritime Organisation
ITU	International Telecommunication Union

link call	call between ships & public telephones via coast radio stations
Mayday	distress call
Mayday Relay	passing on a distress message
MCA or MCGA	Maritime and Coastguard Agency
MMSI	Maritime Mobile Service Identity number
modulation	superimposing a signal onto a radio "carrier" wave
MRAA	Maritime Radio Accounting Authority
MSI	Maritime Safety Information
Navtex	Navigation Teletext for weather forecasts and navigational warnings
Ofcom	Office of Communications
Panpan	urgency call requesting assistance
private channels	for governments to allocate as they think fit
prowords	correct words to use as part of radio procedure
PTT switch	switch pressed to transmit (Press-To-Talk)
safety calls	calls relating to weather forecasts and navigational warnings
SAR	Search And Rescue
SART	Search And Rescue Transponder
scanner mode	facility for radio to monitor a number of channels in quick succession
Securitay	Procedure word identifying a safety call
seelonce	radio silence (French) requested during distress incident
simplex channel	single-frequency channel
SOLAS	Safety of Life at Sea Convention
squelch	control regulating the sensitivity of a receiver
SRC	Short Range Certificate
Tri Watch	facility for radio to monitor Channel 16 and two other channels
urgency call	call requesting assistance which does not justify Mayday call
VHF	Very High Frequency
wavelength	distance between radio waves

gettheknowledge
RYA books for powerboating

RYA Boat Handling for Sportsboats and RIBs DVD
Jon Mendez

First of a new series of RYA DVDs focusing on key areas of boating skills. Essential to anyone new to powerboating, taking a RYA Powerboat Course or those wanting to perfect their skills.

DVD22

RYA Safety Boat Handbook

Essential reading for anyone involved in dinghy or windsurfer rescue at club level. Includes free DVD.

G16

RYA Introduction to Personal Watercraft

A 'must have' for beginners and those wanting to perfect their skills (formerly RYA Personal Watercraft Practical Course Notes).

G35

RYA Start Powerboating
Jon Mendez

The official course book for Levels 1 and 2 of the RYA National Powerboat Scheme (formerly Powerboat Practical Course Notes).

G48

Introduction to Boat Handling for Sail Power
Rob Gibson

All you need to know to become a competent and relaxed boat handler. Includes manoeuvring, marina work, rafting & anchoring.

G68

To find out more about RYA Publications or to place an order, please visit **www.rya.org.uk/shop** or call **0845 345 0372**

gettheknowledge

RYA

MEMBERSHIP

Promoting and Protecting Boating

www.rya.org.uk

IT'S ALL ABOUT YOU AND THE BOATING YOU DO

RYA MEMBERSHIP APPLICATION

RYA
Be part of it

One of boating's biggest attractions is its freedom from rules and regulations. As an RYA member you'll play an active part in keeping it that way, as well as benefiting from free expert advice and information, plus discounts on a wide range of boating products, charts and publications.

To join the RYA, please complete the application form below and send it to The Membership Department, RYA, RYA House, Ensign Way, Hamble, Southampton, Hampshire SO31 4YA. You can also join online at www.rya.org.uk, or by phoning the membership department on +44 (0) 23 8060 4159. Whichever way you choose to apply, you can save money by paying by Direct Debit. A Direct Debit instruction is on the back of this form.

	Title	Forename	Surname	Gender	Date of Birth
Applicant ❶					D D / M M / Y Y Y Y
Applicant ❷					D D / M M / Y Y Y Y
Applicant ❸					D D / M M / Y Y Y Y
Applicant ❹					D D / M M / Y Y Y Y

Address

Post Code

E-mail Applicant ❶

E-mail Applicant ❷

E-mail Applicant ❸

E-mail Applicant ❹

Home Tel   Day Time Tel   Mobile Tel

Type of membership required (Tick Box)

- **Junior (0-11)** Annual rate £5 or **£5 if paying by Direct Debit**
- **Youth (12-17)** Annual rate £14 or **£11 if paying by Direct Debit**
- **Under 25** Annual rate £25 or **£22 if paying by Direct Debit**
- **Personal** Annual rate £43 or **£39 if paying by Direct Debit**
- **Family*** Annual rate £63 or **£59 if paying by Direct Debit**

Save money by completing the Direct Debit form overleaf

Please number up to three boating interests in order, with number one being your principal interest

- Yacht Racing
- Personal Watercraft
- Powerboat Racing
- Yacht Cruising
- Sportboats & RIBs
- Canal Cruising
- Dinghy Racing
- Windsurfing
- River Cruising
- Dinghy Cruising
- Motor Boating

* Family Membership: 2 adults plus any under 18s all living at the same address. Prices valid until 30/9/2011 One discount voucher is accepted for individual memberships, and two discount vouchers are accepted for family membership.

IMPORTANT In order to provide you with membership benefits the details provided by you on this form and in the course of your membership will be maintained on a database. If you do not wish to receive information on member services and benefits please tick here ☐ By applying for membership of the RYA you agree to be bound by the RYA's standard terms and conditions (copies on request or at www.rya.org.uk)

Signature

Date D D / M M / Y Y Y Y

Source Code

Joining Point Code

GET MORE FROM
YOUR
BOATING
SUPPORT THE
RYA

RYA
Be part of it

PAY BY DIRECT DEBIT – AND SAVE MONEY

Instructions to your Bank or Building Society to pay by Direct Debit

Please fill in the form and send to:

Membership Department, Royal Yachting Association, RYA House, Ensign Way, Hamble, Southampton, Hampshire SO31 4YA.

DIRECT Debit

Name and full postal address of your Bank/Building Society

To the Manager .... Bank/Building Society

Address ....

.... Postcode

Name(s) of Account Holder(s)

Branch Sort Code

☐☐ – ☐☐ – ☐☐

Bank/Building Society Account Number

☐☐☐☐☐☐☐☐

Originator's Identification Number

9	5	5	2	1	3

RYA Membership Number (For office use only)

Instructions to your Bank or Building Society

Please pay Royal Yachting Association Direct Debits from the account detailed in this instruction subject to the safeguards assured by The Direct Debit Guarantee. I understand that this instruction may remain with the Royal Yachting Association and, if so, details will be passed electronically to my Bank/Building Society.

Signature(s)

Date: ☐D☐D / M☐M☐ / Y☐Y☐Y☐Y

Notes

Notes